D1009510

Getting It Straight
What the Research Shows about Homosexuality

Peter Sprigg and Timothy Dailey, Co-Editors

Getting It Straight: What the Research Shows about Homosexuality
ISBN 1-55872-009-X
©2004 by Family Research Council
All rights reserved.

Family Research Council
801 G Street NW, Washington DC 20001

Printed in the United States of America
Art Direction and Design by Kimberly Manning

CONTENTS

Introduction

What This Book Is Not

This is not a book about religion or morality

I mention that only because in discussions about homosexuality, religion (usually portrayed as rigid, intolerant, and outdated) and morality (usually portrayed as utterly arbitrary) are often assumed to be the only possible reasons anyone could have for expressing the slightest disapproval of homosexual behavior.

Facts, science, and scholarship, on the other hand, are often assumed to be firmly on the side of those who would treat homosexuality as simply a normal and healthy variant of human sexuality.

These assumptions are false. One of the purposes of this book is to prove that they are false.

That is not to say that the Family Research Council takes no position regarding the theology or morality of homosexuality. Most major religions of the world have condemned homosexual acts. In particular, the Judeo-Christian tradition, as expressed in the Old and New Testaments of the Bible, stands firmly against homosexual practices. And even apart from any special divine revelation, we believe that the fundamental nature of humanity as male and female (natural law) argues against accepting homosexual acts as either normal or moral. But that is not the subject of this book.

This is also not a book about public policy

Many of the debates about homosexuality in American public life today revolve around specific public policy questions. Was the Supreme Court right to declare sodomy laws unconstitutional? Should "hate crimes" against homosexuals be punished more severely than other violent crimes? Should homosexuals be legally protected from "discrimination" in housing and employment? Should public schools teach "tolerance" of homosexual behavior? Should same-sex couples be allowed to legally marry?

This book offers no answers to any of these questions. Again, that is not to say that the Family Research Council has no position on these issues—on the contrary, we are actively engaged in every one of these debates (and we believe the answer is "no" to all of the above). We also believe that bringing moral and religious values to bear on public policy decisions is no violation of the "separation of church and state." But public policy, like religion and morality, is also not the subject of this book.

What This Book Is

Instead, this is a book about what I mentioned above: facts, science, and scholarship.

We are certainly concerned about the gains homosexuals have made in winning the affirmation, celebration, and subsidization of relationships that we believe are harmful and wrong. But the particular concern that motivates this book is our conviction that many of those gains have come, quite simply, at the expense of the truth.

In other words, much of what "everyone now knows" about homosexuality is simply false. And in many cases, those misconceptions have been deliberately promoted by pro-homosexual activists in order to advance their social and political agenda.

Myths about homosexuality

Here are some key misconceptions—we might even call them "myths"—that this book seeks to dispel:

- *"People are born gay."* If this were true, it would advance the idea that sexual orientation is an innate characteristic, like race; that homosexuals, like African Americans, should be legally protected against "discrimination;" and that disapproval of homosexuality should be as socially stigmatized as racism. However, it is not true. The research shows no convincing evidence that anyone is "born gay" and suggests instead that homosexuality results from a complex mix of developmental factors.

- *"10 percent of the population is gay."* If this were true, it would support the notion that "gay people are everywhere," a significant part of every social institution in the country, and thus commonplace, normal, and nothing to fear. However, it is not true. The research clearly shows that a very small percentage of the population (less than three percent) identify themselves as homosexuals.

- *"Homosexuals are seriously disadvantaged by discrimination."* If this were true, it would support the notion that homosexuals need special protections under the law. However, by two of the most common measures of social disadvantage—education and income—it is not true. The research shows that homosexuals actually have significant higher levels of educational attainment than the general public, while the findings on homosexual incomes are, at worst, mixed.

- *"Homosexuality is harmless."* If this were true, it would support the notion that government has no reason to penalize or otherwise disadvantage people who engage in homosexual behavior. However, it is not true. The research clearly shows that homosexual behavior specifically, and a homosexual lifestyle generally, are associated with serious threats to the physical and mental health of those who engage in them and, by extension, to public health.

- *"Children raised by homosexuals suffer no harm."* If this were true, it would support the notion that even the most distinctively heterosexual institutions of our society—the family and marriage itself— should be open to homosexuals on an equal basis. However, it is not true. The research shows clearly that children do best when raised by a married mother and father and that the homosexual lifestyle is unstable. Research specifically on homosexual parents has been fraught with methodological problems, but such research as there is nevertheless does show differences in the children of homosexuals that should raise concern.

- *"Homosexuals are no more likely to molest children than heterosexuals are."* If this were true, it would support the notion that homosexuals should be allowed to work with children as schoolteachers, Boy Scout leaders, and Big Brothers or Big Sisters. However, it is not true. The research clearly shows that same-sex child sexual abuse (mostly men molesting boys) occurs at rates far higher than adult homosexual behavior, and it strongly suggests that many of those abusers are homosexual in their adult orientation as well.

"Getting It Straight"

The title of this book is, of course, a play on words. "Gay" and "straight" have come to be the colloquial synonyms for "homosexual" and "heterosexual" (more on that in a moment). "Getting it straight," on the other hand, is an expression that means getting the truth, getting the facts, getting them accurately, and getting them without bias. It is our belief that this is precisely what has not happened with respect to homosexuality. Instead, from several of the major institutions of our society (the news media, the entertainment media, and academia), we have gotten a message that is not "straight," but is skewed and biased in a particular direction—a "pro-gay" direction. For too long, we have been "getting it gay," and thus inaccurately; the time has come for "getting it straight," meaning accurately.

If the public (including the media and public officials) can come to a more accurate understanding of what the research shows about homosexuality, it will not necessarily dictate a particular response or resolve the debates about the issue. But it will, we hope, create a more level playing field and provide a more rational basis for future decisions.

Some notes on style

This book is intended primarily as a reference work, not a monograph to be read from beginning to end. It thus relies heavily on bullet points, distinct factual findings, and at some points a question-and-answer format, rather than employing long passages of narrative prose. It also uses extensive quotations from the original sources.

We have chosen to cite the sources directly in the text, rather than using footnotes or endnotes. Although normal academic and publishing style would not require this, we wanted to make it as easy as possible for the reader to see the source of each fact we are citing without the effort of looking it up. We also want readers to be able to evaluate for themselves, on the spot, the credibility of the source for each claim. We are confident this approach will make clear that this book does consist of "what the research shows," and not merely our own opinions.

The reader may note that we have primarily (outside of the title) used the terms "homosexual" and heterosexual," rather than the now-common terms "gay" or "straight." The reasons for this approach are stated well by one of our key sources of research:

- "We have used the terms homosexuality and same-gender sex or sexuality interchangeably....We mean these terms to be taken as descriptive of specific partnerships, practices, or feelings. ...Gay and lesbian as alternative terms referring to sexual patterns have the disadvantage of being associated with a particular historical moment and social (and often political) self-identification. The latter involves issues such as participation in a community and culture that are beyond the current research and its primary focus on the sexual."

  Edward O. Laumann, John H. Gagnon, Robert T. Michael, and Stuart Michaels, *The Social Organization of Sexuality: Sexual Practices in the United States* (Chicago: The University of Chicago Press, 1994), footnote 1, 283.

The above reflects the pattern we use in most of this book. When we use the term "homosexual" as a noun, we are referring to a person who actively engages in sexual relations with persons of the same sex and who explicitly prefers such relations to heterosexual ones. When we use the term "homosexuality," we are usually referring to the practice of engaging in overt sexual acts with persons of the same sex. Homosexuality as a "sexual orientation," meaning the mere psychological state of experiencing sexual attractions toward people of the same sex even in the absence of any overt sexual acts, is relevant only to the chapter on "What Causes Homosexuality," wherein we address the psychological origins of such attractions.

Who should use this book

This book should be a prime first reference for anyone who wants or needs accurate information about homosexuality. Specifically, we hope that journalists, elected officials, teachers, professors, clergy, grassroots activists, and other policy makers and cultural leaders will keep a copy close at hand and refer to it often. You will be able to count on the accuracy of the facts and quotations supplied herein, even if you disagree with our position on the issues.

Other resources

Those interested in a reasoned argument in support of our position on these questions are invited to read or order our publications at our website at *www.frc.org*. I also highly recommend a book on the subject, *Dark Obsession: The Tragedy and Threat of the Homosexual Lifestyle* (Broadman and Holman, 2003), by FRC's own Senior Fellow for Marriage and Family Studies (and co-editor of this work), Timothy J. Dailey.

This book is a companion volume to, and in certain respects modeled after, another publication: *The Family Portrait: A Compilation of Data, Research and Public Opinion on the Family* (Washington: Family Research Council, 2002). These two books constitute the flagship publications of FRC's new Center for Marriage and Family Studies, and our intention is to issue updated editions of each approximately once every two years. Look for the second edition of *The Family Portrait* later in 2004.

Peter Sprigg
Director
Center for Marriage and Family Studies
Family Research Council

Acknowledgements

I wish to express my thanks to the Library of Congress and to the Himmelfarb Health Sciences Library at George Washington University, where much of this research was conducted; to Alan Crippen and Brian Robertson of the Family Research Council for their support of this project (and their patience); and to Witherspoon Fellows Joshua Grissom, Anna Hanger, Clinton Sievers, and Joshua Stock. Without the long hours they spent searching in libraries and transcribing quotations from sources, this project would still be far from complete.

Peter Sprigg
Family Research Council

CHAPTER I

What Causes Homosexuality?

This is the first and perhaps the most basic question about homosexuality. In order to understand the phenomenon of same-sex sexual relations, we must first explore what the research shows about the origins of such attractions.

There are two main theories as to what causes homosexual attractions. One is that a homosexual orientation is essentially dictated by genetic and or biological factors—put simply, that people are "born gay." The other theory is that homosexual attractions develop as primarily as a result of psychological and environmental influences and early experiences. In the public square, the latter theory has appeared to be in decline and the former gaining favor in recent decades. But what does the research show? Let's look at these two theories in turn.

Are People "Born Gay?"

While the research of the infamous sex researcher Alfred Kinsey is often used by those seeking the moral approval of homosexuality, there is one point on which he is seldom quoted: his rejection of a biological origin for homosexuality.

- Kinsey's colleague and biographer, Wardell Pomeroy, reports: "By the end of 1940 he had recorded more than 450 homosexual histories, enough to convince him that the psychologists were making matters worse by starting with the assumption that homosexuality was an inherited abnormality which could not be cured simply because it was inherent. Kinsey was convinced that there was absolutely no evidence of inheritance."

Wardell B. Pomeroy, *Dr. Kinsey and the Institute for Sex Research* (New York: Harper & Row, 1972), 76.

Alleged evidence of the biological origin of homosexuality

A handful of studies published during the 1990s have claimed to offer evidence in favor of a biological or genetic cause for homosexuality. Three of these in particular—a study of brain structure by Simon LeVay, a study of twins by J. Michael Bailey and Richard C. Pillard, and a study of "gene linkage" and "gene markers" by a team led by Dean H. Hamer—attracted considerable media attention and are largely responsible for the popular belief that a "gay gene" has already been found. Let's look at these in turn.

The Brain Studies of Simon LeVay

Some researchers have theorized that the sexual preferences and behavior of homosexuals may be dictated by the structure of the brain—particularly if the brains of homosexual men, for example, can be shown to resemble those of heterosexual women more than they resemble those of heterosexual men.

One highly publicized study that purported to demonstrate this was conducted in 1991 by former Salk Institute researcher Simon LeVay. LeVay studied the brains of cadavers, including 18 men known to have been homosexual and one known to have been bisexual. He compared them with the brains of another 16 men and six women whom he presumed to have been heterosexual. This is what LeVay claimed to have found:

- "INAH 3 was more than twice as large in the heterosexual men as in the women. It was also, however, more than twice as large in the heterosexual men as in the homosexual men. This finding indicates that INAH is dimorphic with sexual orientation [i.e., shows a difference in structure between homosexuals and heterosexuals], at least in men, and suggests that sexual orientation has a biological substrate."

  Simon LeVay, "A Difference in Hypothalamic Structure Between Heterosexual and Homosexual Men," *Science*, 253: 1034 (August 1991).

Weaknesses of LeVay's study

- LeVay's study, however, suffered from serious methodological errors, including the failure to adequately identify a control group. LeVay made questionable assumptions regarding the orientation of the "heterosexual" cadavers. He assumed that they were all heterosexual, even though a number of the allegedly "heterosexual" subjects had died of AIDS, a disease that remains far more common among homosexual men than among heterosexuals: "Sixteen subjects were presumed to be heterosexual men: six of these subjects died of AIDS and ten of other causes."

LeVay, "A Difference in Hypothalamic Structure Between Heterosexual and Homosexual Men," 1035.

- Another anomaly of LeVay's study was the fact that three of the "heterosexuals" had brain clusters smaller than the mean size for the homosexuals. On the other hand, three of the homosexuals had larger clusters than the mean size for "heterosexuals." Thus, LeVay was forced to admit, "The existence of 'exceptions' in the present sample (that is, presumed heterosexual men with small INAH 3 nuclei, and homosexual men with large ones) hints at the possibility that sexual orientation, although an important variable, may not be the sole determinant of INAH 3 size."

Ibid.

- LeVay, in fact, admitted that his claim of a *correlation* between this brain structure and sexual orientation could not prove *causation*, or even the direction of influence, noting that "[T]he results do not allow one to decide if the size of INAH 3 in an individual is the cause or consequence of that individual's sexual orientation, or if the size of INAH 3 and sexual orientation co-vary under the influence of some third, unidentified variable."

Ibid.

- All 19 of his homosexual subjects had died of AIDS, and LeVay noted that another "problem" was "the possibility that AIDS patients constitute an unrepresentative subset of gay men, characterized, for example, by a tendency to engage in sexual relations with large numbers of different partners or by a strong preference for the receptive role in anal intercourse," both of which are major risk factors in acquiring human immunodeficiency virus (HIV) infection.

Ibid.

- A related issue is that the allegedly smaller brain clusters might not have caused homosexuality, but instead could have resulted from sexual activity or AIDS-related brain damage. "[T]here is the possibility that the small size of INAH 3 in the homosexual men is the result of AIDS or its complications and is not related to the men's sexual orientation." He further allowed that until "tissue from homosexual men dying of other causes becomes available, the possibility that the small size of INAH 3 in these men reflects a disease effect that is peculiar to homosexual AIDS patients cannot be rigorously excluded."

Ibid., 1036.

Other researchers reject LeVay's findings

- William Byne and Bruce Parsons, writing in *Archives of General Psychiatry*, also raised the question of how AIDS could have impacted LeVay's subjects, concluding that it is possible to "hypothesize a plausible mechanism by which human immunodeficiency virus infection" could account for a selective reduction in the volume of INAH3 in the homosexual men.

- Byne and Parsons also challenge LeVay's use of animal studies "to support the notion that the INAH3 is crucial to the 'generation of male-typical sexual behavior.'"

- Finally, they conclude that "LeVay's study can be faulted for a number of technical flaws, such as a variable method of tissue fixation, inadequate sexual histories, and small sample sizes."

William Byne and Bruce Parsons, "Human Sexual Orientation: The Biologic Theories Reappraised," *Archives of General Psychiatry*, 50: 235 (March 1993).

Other Brain Studies

Theories concerning the anterior commissure

Since LeVay, researchers have examined other areas of the brain to see if there are differences between homosexuals and heterosexuals.

- One study by L. S. Allen and R. A. Gorski (1991) reported that an area of the brain known as the anterior commissure (AC) "was larger in homosexual as opposed to heterosexual men, a finding that was interpreted as support for the hypothesis that sexual orientation reflects the sexually differentiated state of the brain."

• However, after reviewing the evidence, researchers Mitchell S. Lasco, et al., reported: "We examined the cross-sectional area of the AC in postmortem material from 120 individuals, and found no variation in the size of the AC with age, HIV status, sex, or sexual orientation."

Mitchell S. Lasco, Theresa J. Jordan, Mark A. Edgar, Carol K. Petito, and William Byne, "A Lack of Dimorphism of Sex or Sexual Orientation in the Human Anterior Commissure," *Brain Research*, 936 (2002): 95.

• Byne and Parsons add that even if Allen and Gorski's findings *could* be replicated, "the size of the AC alone would tell us nothing about an individual's sexual orientation because the overlap of AC size between homosexual and heterosexual men was tremendous (i.e., the size of the AC of 27 of 30 homosexual men fell within the range established by 30 heterosexual men). Because these authors relied heavily on the brains of the subjects with acquired immuno-deficiency syndrome and provide little clinical history, their study is subject to many of the same interpretive difficulties as LeVay's study of the hypothalmus."

Byne and Parsons, "Human Sexual Orientation: The Biologic Theories Reappraised," 235.

The suprachiasmatic nucleus

Byne and Parsons also reject as unsubstantiated a report indicating that the size of another hypothalamic nucleus, the suprachiasmatic nucleus (SCN), is larger in homosexual than heterosexual men:

• "Again, however, this study has not been corroborated, and few studies of this sort have proved to be replicable in the past. But even if corroborated, this finding would not support the prenatal hormonal hypothesis, because in humans the size of the SCN does not vary with sex. Furthermore, existing evidence does not suggest a primary role for the SCN in the regulation of sexual behaviors."

Ibid.

The corpus callosum

Byne and Parsons mention yet another attempt to prove that the brain structure of homosexuals differs from that of heterosexuals:

- "There has also been recent speculation that the morphology of the corpus callosum may be found to be female-typical in homosexual men (LeVay. *New York Times.* October 7, 1991: letter). Such speculation is premature as the 23 studies that have sought sexual dimorphism [i.e., differences between men and women] in the corpus callosum have yielded conflicting results. Although the initial study…concluded that the splenium of the corpus callosum is larger (P=.08) and more bulbous in women than in men, none of the 22 subsequent studies replicated the sex difference in splenial size. Furthermore, while some researchers did replicate the finding of a more bulbous splenium in women, others found it more bulbous in men and still others found no sex difference. As described by Byne, some of the negative studies have been unfortunately misinterpreted as successful replications."

  Byne and Parsons, "Human Sexual Orientation: The Biologic Theories Reappraised," 235.

Conclusion: Brain Studies

- Byne and Parsons conclude: "In summary, three as yet uncorroborated reports suggest that the size of three different brain structures may vary with sexual orientation in men. These reports must be viewed cautiously while replication studies are pending." The authors note further that even if these inconclusive findings were consistently replicated, "we will not know whether the anatomic correlates are a cause or a consequence of sexual orientation."

  Ibid., 229, 235.

The Bailey and Pillard Study of Twins

- Writing in the *Archives of General Psychiatry*, J. Michael Bailey and Richard C. Pillard claim to have found a higher rate of homosexuality among identical ("monozygotic") and fraternal ("dizygotic") twins than among adoptive siblings. They reported that "of the relatives whose sexual orientation could be rated, 52 percent (29/56) of monozygotic cotwins, 22 percent (12/54) of dizygotic cotwins, and 11 percent (6/57) of adoptive brothers were homosexual..." The authors concluded that "the pattern of rates of homosexuality by type of relative was generally consistent with substantial genetic influence..."

J. Michael Bailey and Richard C. Pillard, "A Genetic Study of Male Sexual Orientation," *Archives of General Psychiatry*, 48 (December 1991): 1089, 1094.

The findings of Bailey and Pillard, however, are not entirely consistent with a genetic theory.

Methodological deficiencies of Bailey and Pillard

- Bailey and Pillard themselves alluded to problems with their sampling method: "The sampling method employed in this study falls short of the ideal genetic epidemiological study, which would involve systematic sampling from a well-specified population. In particular, although all recruiting advertisements stated that [subjects] were desired regardless of the sexual orientation of their relatives, there is no guarantee that volunteers heeded this request."

Bailey and Pillard, "A Genetic Study of Male Sexual Orientation," 1094.

- Byne and Parsons confirm that Bailey and Pillard did not employ "a systematically ascertained sample of twins. Subjects...were recruited through advertisements placed in homosexual-oriented periodicals and, therefore, may not be typical of the homosexual population at large."

Byne and Parsons, "Human Sexual Orientation: The Biologic Theories Reappraised," 230.

Twin study fails to support genetic hypothesis

- As Byne and Parsons explain, in Bailey and Pillard's study, "the concordance rate for homosexuality in nontwin biologic brothers was only 9.2 percent—significantly lower than that required by a simple genetic hypothesis, which, on the basis of shared genetic material, would predict similar concordance rates for dizygotic twins and nontwin biologic brothers. Furthermore, the fact that the concordance rates were similar for nontwin biologic brothers (9.2 percent) and genetically unrelated adoptive brothers (11.0 percent) is at odds with a simple genetic hypothesis, which would predict a higher concordance rate for biologic siblings."

Byne and Parsons, "Human Sexual Orientation: The Biologic Theories Reappraised," 229.

• Bailey and Pillard themselves admit that the rate of homosexuality among nontwin biological siblings, as reported by the subjects, was "significantly lower than would be predicted by a simple genetic hypothesis and other published reports."

Bailey and Pillard, "A Genetic Study of Male Sexual Orientation," 1089.

• In their analysis, Byne and Parsons point out that the evidence actually suggests an environmental rather than a genetic cause for homosexuality, arguing that "we must at least consider the possibility that the higher concordance rate for homosexuality in dizygotic twins compared with nontwin biologic brothers is due to increased similarity of the trait-relevant environment in the former. This is because dizygotic twins and full biologic siblings share the same proportion of genetic material. Thus, any difference in the true concordance rates would be attributable to environmental rather than genetic factors."

Byne and Parsons, "Human Sexual Orientation: The Biologic Theories Reappraised," 229–30.

Other twin studies fail to support the genetic theory

• A study in *The Journal of Sex Research* examined monozygotic and dizygotic twins in the Minnesota Twin Registry. While the study claimed to find "significant genetic effects" for the sexual orientation of women, no such effects were found for men: "For men, no significant genetic effects were found for number of opposite- and same-sex sexual encounters, nor for sexual orientation."

Scott L. Hershberger, "A Twin Registry Study of Male and Female Sexual Orientation," *The Journal of Sex Research*, 34 (2): 212 (1997).

• The study concluded that environmental factors were a primary component of the formation of sexual orientation: "Special sibling environment effects were found for self-identified sexual orientation for male and female MZ [monozygotic] twins and opposite-sex female DZ [dizygotic] twins." The authors concluded, "Environmental effects were also important for sexual orientation, in fact, more important in the aggregate than genetic effects..."

Hershberger, "A Twin Registry Study of Male and Female Sexual Orientation," 220, 221.

- Bailey and Pillard themselves note other twin studies that were unable to demonstrate a genetic cause: "Buhrich et al reported a twin study of sexual orientation and related behaviors...They found a strong familial resemblance, but had insufficient power to determine whether that correlation was due to genetic or environmental factors or both."

Bailey and Pillard, "A Genetic Study of Male Sexual Orientation," *Archives of General Psychiatry*, 1090.

- Miron Baron, writing in the *British Medical Journal*, also questioned the results of the twin studies that have been conducted: "Most of these results are uninterpretable because of small samples or unresolved questions about phenotypic classification, the selection of cases, and the diagnosis of twin zygosity or because they make the untested assumption that monozygotic and dizygotic twins have similar environmental experiences such that any difference in concordance rate would be genetic in origin." Baron concluded: [T]he finding that the adoptive brothers of homosexual twins are more prone to homosexuality than the biological siblings suggests that male homosexuality may well be environmental."

Miron Baron, "Genetic linkage and male homosexual orientation," *BMJ*, 307: 337 (7 August 1993).

- If homosexuality were a trait determined entirely by a person's genes, one would expect 100 percent of the identical (monozygotic or MZ) twins of homosexuals to also be homosexual. Yet this is not the case; indeed, "what is most intriguing" about the twins studies to Byne and Parsons "is the large proportion of MZ twins who were discordant for homosexuality despite sharing not only their genes but also their prenatal and familial environments. The large proportion of discordant pairs underscores our ignorance of the factors that are involved, and the manner in which they interact, in the emergence of sexual orientation."

Byne and Parsons, "Human Sexual Orientation: The Biologic Theories Reappraised," 230.

Gene Studies of Dean Hamer

A flurry of media reports in 1993 indicated that scientists had at long last discovered a "gay gene." The reports were based on the work of geneticist Dean Hamer of the National Cancer Institute. Hamer, however, never claimed to have found a gene that inevitably determines that a person will be homosexual. Rather, he claimed to have located a genetic component to some instances of male homosexuality.

Dean H. Hamer, *et al.*, "A Linkage Between DNA Markers on the X Chromosome and Male Sexual Orientation," *Science* 261 (1993): 321–327.

• Hamer writes: "The role of genetics in male sexual orientation was investigated by pedigree and linkage analyses on 114 families of homosexual men….The goal of our work was to determine whether or not male sexual orientation is genetically influenced. We used the standard techniques of modern human genetics, namely pedigree analysis and family DNA linkage studies."

Hamer, *et al.*, "A Linkage Between DNA Markers on the X Chromosome and Male Sexual Orientation," 321.

Of the families Hamer interviewed that had more than one son who was homosexual, a significantly larger number had a maternal uncle or a maternal aunt's son who was also homosexual. By comparison, the links with paternal linkage were weaker. This would suggest a maternal linkage for male homosexuality in some cases. Finding homosexual brothers who had homosexual maternal uncles would indicate that the gene determining homosexuality was transmitted through the mother's family line.

After studying 40 pairs of brothers who were homosexual, Hamer hypothesized that a certain genetic marker on the X chromosome was at least partially responsible for their homosexuality. Since men have an X and a Y chromosome, and they inherit their X chromosome from their mothers, Hamer theorized that the mother may be the carrier of the gene determining homosexuality in their sons. Homosexual behavior would not be manifested in the mothers' lives, but they would pass that gene on to their sons.

Hamer's study is known as "linkage" study, where researchers isolate traits found in an extended family and then looks for a common DNA segment, or marker, on a particular chromosome. If the same marker is present consistently in the family members who have that trait, it is theorized that the marker may be the gene that causes—or "codes"—for that trait. Linkage studies have successfully located genes that cause Huntington's disease, cystic fibrosis, and muscular dystrophy. However, to date linkage studies have not found genes that code for complex behaviors.

Hamer's findings

- Hamer claimed: "We have now produced evidence that one form of male homosexuality is preferentially transmitted through the maternal side and is genetically linked to chromosomal region Xq28....[I]t appears that Xq28 contains a gene that contributes to homosexual orientation in males."

Hamer, *et al.*, "A Linkage Between DNA Markers on the X Chromosome and Male Sexual Orientation," 325.

What did Hamer not find?

- Hamer did not claim to have found that homosexuality is directly inherited, like eye color: "Although the observed rates of homosexual orientation in the maternally derived uncles and male cousins of gay men were higher than in female and paternally related male relatives, they were lower than would be expected for a simple Mendelian trait."

- In addition, Hamer did not claim that all cases of homosexuality could be explained by the presence of this gene marker: "[T]here was a substantial number of families in which lesbians or paternally related gay men were present. This could be explained if some instances of homosexuality were male-limited and maternally inherited whereas others were either sporadic, not sex-limited, or not maternally transmitted."

Ibid., 322.

- In fact, Hamer did not even attempt to estimate what proportion of the instances of homosexuality could be linked to this gene marker: "At present, we can say nothing about the fraction of all instances of male homosexuality that are related or unrelated to the Xq28 candidate locus..."

Ibid., 325.

- He furthermore admitted the influence of environmental factors: "Given the overall complexity of human sexuality, it is not surprising that a single genetic locus does not account for all of the observed variability. Sib-pairs that are discordant at Xq28 should provide a useful resource for identifying additional genes or environmental, experiential, or cultural factors (or some combination of these) that influence the development of male sexual orientation."

Hamer, *et al.*, "A Linkage Between DNA Markers on the X Chromosome and Male Sexual Orientation," 325–26.

Linkage studies of other traits give reasons for caution

- Baron summarizes: "There are lessons too from other studies—for example, of the hypothesis that another behavioural trait, manic depressive illness, is X linked. Support for this hypothesis was initially furnished by segregation patterns consistent with X linked transmission and reports of linkage to chromosomal region Xq27-28. In some studies the statistical support for these findings far exceeded the significance levels reported by Hamer *et al*. Moreover, the evidence from twin and adoption studies for a genetic component in manic depressive illness was far more compelling than that for homosexuality. Unfortunately, non-replication of the linkage findings by other investigators, as well as extension and reevaluation of the original data, has resulted in diminished support for this hypothesis. This outcome underscores the uncertainties in linkage studies of complex behavioural traits."

Miron Baron, "Genetic linkage and male homosexual orientation," *BMJ*, 307: 338 (7 August 1993).

- George Rice, et al., writing in *Science*, notes that "the evidence for X linkage has been questioned on theoretical and empirical grounds (8, 9). Most would agree that male homosexual orientation is not a simple Mendelian trait. There would be strong selective pressures against such a gene. Hamer's identification of a contribution from a gene near Xq28 to homosexuality in some families that were selected for X-linked transmission of that trait might be fraught with type 1 (false positive) error. This is important to consider, given the irreproducibility of many linkage reports for complex behavioral traits."

George Rice, Carol Anderson, Neil Risch, and George Ebers, "Male Homosexuality: Absence of Linkage to Microsatellite Markers at Xq28," *Science*, 284: 666 (April 1999).

Hamer's findings have not been replicated

- The 1999 study in *Science* by Rice, et al., attempted without success to duplicate Hamer's findings. "Sharing of alleles at position Xq28 was studied in 52 gay male sibling pairs from Canadian families. Four markers at Xq28 were analyzed....Allele and haplotype sharing for these markers was not increased over expectation. These results do not support an X-linked gene underlying male homosexuality."

  Rice, *et al.*, "Male Homosexuality: Absence of Linkage to Microsatellite Markers at Xq28," 665.

- The authors write: "It is unclear why our results are so discrepant from Hamer's original study (6). Because our study was larger than that of Hamer *et al.*, we certainly had adequate power to detect a genetic effect as large as was reported in that study. Nonetheless, our data do not support the presence of a gene of large effect influencing sexual orientation at position Xq28."

  Ibid., 667.

A key problem: If homosexuality were genetic, it would have died out

- Baron explains a key objection to "gay gene" theories: "Support for a genetic hypothesis is further complicated by cultural and evolutionary considerations....Sexual patterns are to some extent a product of society's expectations, but it would be difficult to envisage a change in the prevalence of a genetic trait merely in response to changing cultural norms. Also, from an evolutionary perspective, genetically determined homosexuality would have become extinct long ago because of reduced reproduction. Thus the purported linkage stands in apparent contradiction to the flimsy genetic and epidemiological evidence....[A] single gene or a particular genetic mechanism is unlikely to explain most of the variance in a phenomenon as complex as sexual orientation. Whether or not this sample is truly representative of familial homosexuality is an open question."

  Miron Baron, "Genetic linkage and male homosexual orientation," *BMJ*, 307: 337 (7 August 1993).

- Bem also discusses the theory that homosexuality is "an evolutionary anomaly," and asks the question: "How do lesbians and gay men manage to pass on their gene pool to successive generations? Several

hypothetical scenarios have been offered....Although these specula-
tions have been faulted on theoretical, metatheoretical, and empirical
grounds (Futuyma & Risch, 1983/84), a more basic problem with
such arguments is their circularity. As Bleier has noted about similar
accounts, this logic makes a *premise* of the genetic basis of behaviors,
then cites a certain animal or human behavior, constructs a speculative story to explain how the behavior (if it were genetically based)
could have served or could serve to maximize the reproductive success of the individual, and this conjecture then becomes evidence for
the *premise* that the behavior was genetically determined. (1984, p.
17)"

Daryl J. Bem, "Exotic Becomes Erotic: A Developmental Theory of Sexual Orientation," *Psychological Review*, 103 (2): 328–29 (1996).

Theories that Hormone Levels Influence Sexual Orientation

The theory that homosexuality was the result of a deficiency of male sex hormones in male homosexuals and, conversely, excessive levels of testosterone in
lesbians, was repeatedly raised from the 1940s through the late 1970s.

- Byne and Parsons note that such ideas persisted "despite the failure
  of hormone treatments to influence sexual orientation and despite
  the fact that most studies failed to find any association between adult
  hormone levels and sexual orientation."

  Byne and Parsons, "Human Sexual Orientation: The Biologic Theories Reappraised," 228.

Prenatal hormone levels

When research data failed to support this theory, attention turned from adult
hormonal levels to the levels of hormones in the womb.

- Bem explains that, reasoning from research on rats, "some researchers
  hypothesized that human males who are exposed prenatally to substantially lower than average amounts of testosterone and human
  females who are exposed to substantially higher than average
  amounts of testosterone will be predisposed toward a homosexual
  orientation in adult life."

  Bem, "Exotic Becomes Erotic: A Developmental Theory of Sexual Orientation," 329.

However, other researchers questioned comparing hormonal levels in rats with humans.

- Byne and Parsons explain: "The problems inherent in extrapolating from mating behaviors and postures in rodents to psychological processes in humans are complex....Motivated sexual behaviors in humans are unlikely to be under such rigid endocrine control. Thus, the suitability of...behavior in rodents as a model for motivated sexual behavior in humans is questionable....It is difficult to imagine that the gamut and plasticity of human sexual behavior can be reduced to factors as simple" as the way in which a female rat responds to a male.

  Byne and Parsons, "Human Sexual Orientation: The Biologic Theories Reappraised," 231.

- Other researchers claimed to find a link between prenatal hormonal levels and lesbianism by interviewing women who have congenital adrenal hyperplasia (CAH), a chronic endocrine disorder that exposes them to abnormally high levels of androgen during the prenatal period—levels comparable to those received by males during gestation. According to Bem, "CAH women have now reported more bisexual or homosexual responsiveness than control women."

  Bem, "Exotic Becomes Erotic: A Developmental Theory of Sexual Orientation," 329.

However, other researchers question any direct link between prenatal hormones to sexual orientation:

- Bem notes that both boys and girls who were exposed to abnormally high levels of angrogen during gestation exhibited "increased aggression later in childhood (Reinisch, 1981), and girls with CAH have shown stronger preferences for male-typical activities and male playmates in childhood than control girls." Thus, according to Bem, "the major reason for expecting CAH girls to be disproportionately homoerotic in adulthood is that they are overwhelmingly likely to feel different from other girls. Not only are they gender nonconforming in their play activities and peer preferences, as most lesbians are during their childhood years, but the salience of the CAH status itself aids and abets their perception of being different from other girls on gender-relevant dimensions."

  Ibid., 329–30.

- Byne and Parsons summarize the available evidence: "[I]f the prenatal hormonal hypothesis is correct, then one might expect to find homosexuality in a large proportion of males with syndromes involving prenatal androgen deficiency or insensitivity, and also in females with syndromes involving androgen excess. However, extensive reviews of the literature suggest that this is not the case." They conclude: "Currently, data pertaining to possible neurochemical differences between homosexual and heterosexual individuals are lacking."

Byne and Parsons, "Human Sexual Orientation: The Biologic Theories Reappraised," 230–32.

Genetic Characteristics May Play an Indirect Role in Sexual Orientation

To date, all theories regarding the existence a "gay gene" remain unsubstantiated. However, some researchers suggest that genetics may play an indirect role through the presence of certain temperamental traits that increase the likelihood that certain individuals will experience same-sex attractions or come to identify themselves as homosexual.

- Byne and Parsons explain: "For example, if a gene influenced some factor, such as temperament, in a manner that would increase the probability of homosexual development in a particular environment, that gene could be called a gene for homosexuality with reduced penetrance." However, the authors caution: "Such terminology, however, would minimize the overriding importance of environment in such a scenario."

  Ibid., 230.

- Bem agrees that "biological factors influence sexual orientation only indirectly, by intervening earlier in the chain of events to determine a child's temperaments and subsequent activity preferences.... [C]orrelation between a biological factor and sexual orientation is more plausibly attributed to its influence in early childhood than to a direct link with sexual orientation."

  Bem, "Exotic Becomes Erotic: A Developmental Theory of Sexual Orientation," 327.

Much of the confusion about what research has actually shown regarding a genetic influence on the development of homosexuality has to do with a misunderstanding of the difference between a trait that is "heritable" (that is, one that runs in families) and one that is "inherited" (that is, one which is directly determined by genes). The difference, and the multiple pathways that could lead to homosexuality, were acknowledged by Bailey and Pillard of the twin studies:

- "Heritability is not informative regarding the development of sexual orientation (or, for that matter, of any trait). That is, given any heritability estimate, there are a variety of possible developmental mechanisms. For instance, these data are consistent with heritable variation in prenatal brain development or in some aspect of physical appearance that, by way of differential parental treatment, leads to differences in sexual orientation....[O]ne assumption of the heritability analyses presented above is that *there are no major genes for homosexuality...*" [emphasis added].

J. Michael Bailey and Richard C. Pillard, "A Genetic Study of Male Sexual Orientation," *Archives of General Psychiatry*, 48: 1095 (December 1991).

Biological theories of homosexuality

- Byne and Parsons conclude that the biologic theory remains unproven, and note that "the appeal of current biologic explanations for sexual orientation may derive more from dissatisfaction with the present status of psychosocial explanations than from a substantiating body of experimental data. Critical review shows the evidence favoring a biologic theory to be lacking. In an alternative model, temperamental and personality traits interact with the familial and social milieu as the individual's sexuality emerges. Because such traits may be heritable or developmentally influenced by hormones, the model predicts an apparent nonzero heritability for homosexuality without requiring that either genes or hormones directly influence sexual orientation per se."

Byne and Parsons, "Human Sexual Orientation: The Biologic Theories Reappraised," 228.

- Bem concurs that "a theoretical rationale for a direct path between the genotype and sexual orientation has not even been clearly articulated, let alone established."

Bem, "Exotic Becomes Erotic: A Developmental Theory of Sexual Orientation," 328.

The Political Agenda Behind Promoting the "Gay Gene"

- Revealingly, Byne and Parsons note: "Finally, political arguments have been offered in favor of biologic causation. It has been suggested that if sexual orientation is largely a biologic phenomenon, 'society would do well to reexamine its expectations of those who cannot conform'; and, writing in the 'Opinions and Editorials' pages of the *New York Times* (December 17, 1991: 19), Bailey and Pillard stated: 'If true, a biological explanation is good news for homosexuals and their advocates.' However, political arguments have no impact on biologic realities, including the extent of genetic or hormonal influences on the emergence of sexual orientation."

Byne and Parsons, "Human Sexual Orientation: The Biologic Theories Reappraised," 236.

How the media distort the issue

- Bem refers to the role that the media play in distorting the scientific evidence and misleadingly assuming that there exists a "gay gene": "Like all well-bred scientists, biologically oriented researchers in the field of sexual orientation dutifully murmur the mandatory mantra that correlation is not cause. But the reductive temptation of biological causation is so seductive that the caveat cannot possibly compete with the excitement of discovering yet another link between the anatomy of our brains and the anatomy of our lovers' genitalia. Unfortunately, the caveat vanishes completely as word of the latest discovery moves from *Science* to *Newsweek*. The public can be forgiven for believing that research is but one government grant away from pinpointing the [sexual] preference gene."

Bem, "Exotic Becomes Erotic: A Developmental Theory of Sexual Orientation," 330.

Do Upbringing, Experience, and the Social Environment Contribute to the Development of Homosexuality?

In 1973 the American Psychiatric Association removed homosexuality from its list of mental disorders. That decision did not come as a result of new research. Ronald Bayer, author of the most exhaustive treatment of the 1973 decision, has described what actually happened:

- "A furious egalitarianism that challenged every instance of authority had compelled psychiatric experts to negotiate the pathological status of homosexuality with homosexuals themselves. The result was not a conclusion based on an approximation of the scientific truth as dictated by reason, but was instead an action demanded by the ideological temper of the times."

  Ronald Bayer, *Homosexuality and American Psychiatry: The Politics of Diagnosis* (Princeton, NJ: Princeton University Press, 1987), 3.

Prior to 1973 an extensive literature existed on the role of upbringing and experience in the development of homosexuality. Yet one of the unfortunate effects of the APA decision was to largely stifle further research on the psychological origins of homosexuality.

In the remainder of this chapter we will examine parts of that large body of work showing the key developmental influences, as well as looking at more recent research supporting developmental theories of homosexuality.

Early childhood developmental factors

The causes of same-sex attraction are many and varied. Prior to 1973 many researchers focused on the early childhood years:

- A 1969 study in the *Journal of Consulting and Clinical Psychology* concluded: "We found a remarkable number of conditions and circumstances that may result in homosexuality....What happens after the child is born is complicated by many factors; there are not only inner biological and emotional factors, parental and familial surroundings, social and cultural circumstances; but the various pressures and expectations shift as the child grows and hardens as he establishes his ways into his eventual adult character structure."

  Ralph H. Gundlach, "Childhood Parental Relationships and the Establishment of Gender Roles of Homosexuals," *Journal of Consulting and Clinical Psychology*, 33 (April 1969): 137.

- Similarly, Psychiatrists Byne and Parsons, writing in *Archives of General Psychiatry*, state that "it seems reasonable to suggest that the stage for future sexual orientation may be set by experiences during early development, perhaps the first 4 years of life." The authors conclude: "The inadequacies of present psychosocial explanations do not justify turning to biology by default—especially when, at present, the biologic alternatives seem to have no greater explanatory value.

In fact, the current trend may be to underrate the explanatory power of extant psychosocial models."

William Byne and Bruce Parsons, "Human Sexual Orientation: The Biologic Theories Reappraised," *Archives of General Psychiatry*, 50 (March 1993): 236.

• Back in 1968 Ralph R. Greenson, clinical professor of psychiatry at UCLA, offered the following developmental theory, which focuses on the need of boys to "dis-identify" from their mother: [T]he male child, in order to attain a healthy sense of maleness, must replace the primary object of his identification, the mother, and must identify instead with the father. I believe it is the difficulties inherent in this additional step of development, from which girls are exempt, which are responsible for certain special problems in the man's gender identity, his sense of belonging to the male sex....The male child's ability to dis-identify will determine the success or failure of his later identification with his father."

Ralph R. Greenson, "Dis-Identifying From Mother: Its Special Importance for the Boy," *International Journal of Psychoanalysis*, 49 (1968): 370.

Parental influence

Another focus of researchers has been how the personality traits of the parents may contribute to same-sex attraction, Theories about how a child's relationship with his or her parent can effect homosexual feelings can be traced in the psychiatric literature going back nearly a century:

• According to the *Archives of Sexual Behavior* "Freud (1916) described the mothers of homosexuals as excessively loving and their fathers as retiring or absent. Stekel (1930) noted strong, dominant mothers and weak fathers. In 1936, Terman and Miles found the mothers of homosexuals to be especially demonstrative, affectionate, and emotional, while the fathers were typically unsympathetic, autocratic, or frequently away from home."

Marvin Siegelman, "Parental Background of Male Homosexuals and Heterosexuals," *Archives of Sexual Behavior*, 3 (1974): 3-4.

• Similarly, the *Bulletin of the Menninger Clinic* noted the following from a review of the literature back in 1963: "Bender and Paster in a study of 19 actively homosexual children, found either a grossly deficient or very negative relationship with the same-sex parent, coupled with an overly intimate attachment to the opposite-sex parent."

- "And, in a recent publication by West, a number of contemporary investigators are cited who independently have reached the same conclusion concerning the mother-son factor in male homosexuality. In this same publication, West presents his own study in England of 50 homosexual males and 50 matched control (nonhomosexual) males. His findings clearly show that male homosexuals are much more likely to come from a family constellation involving an overintense mother and unsatisfactory father relationship."

Daniel G. Brown, "Homosexuality and Family Dynamics," *Bulletin of the Menninger Clinic* 27 (5): 229–30 (Sept. 1963).

The Work of Irving Bieber

A study conducted by a team of researchers headed by Irving Bieber, published as a book in 1962, is still considered a landmark in the field. Bieber, an influential researcher in the field of the etiology of homosexuality in the 1960s, summarized the team's findings this way:

- "The 'classical' homosexual triangular pattern is one where the mother is CBI [close-binding-intimate] with the son and is dominant and minimizing toward a husband who is a detached father, particularly a hostile-detached one. From our statistical analysis, the chances appear to be high that any son exposed to this parental combination will become homosexual or develop severe homosexual problems.'"

Irving Bieber et al., *Homosexuality: A Psychoanalytical Study* (New York: Vintage Books, 1962), 172.

- Subsequent studies confirmed Bieber's findings. In 1964 a British psychiatrist compared his patients who were either homosexuals or neurotic heterosexuals, and reported that "approximately 70 percent of the homosexuals (62 percent plus one-third of 28 percent) were either over-attached to their mother or did not get on well with their father."

P. J. O'Connor, "Aetiological Factors in Homosexuality as Seen in Royal Air Force Psychiatric Practice," *British Journal of Psychiatry*, 110 (May 1964): 384–85.

- A 1965 study of homosexual college students in *Genetic Psychology*

Monographs also generally confirmed Bieber's work: "Our findings are similar. Whereas the percent of close-binding-intimate mothers was 55 for the Homosexuals, the corresponding percent for the Controls was only 20." In addition, "Bieber *et al.* found a little less than twice as many detached-hostile and detached-indifferent fathers among their Homosexuals as compared with their control group. We had 42 percent detached fathers for the Homosexuals and 24 percent for the Controls. Whereas in Bieber's study most of the fathers were detached and *hostile*, our trend was that the fathers were rather detached and *indifferent*. The present authors feel that the function of the *detached* father in the psychogenesis of male homosexuality deserves a more important place than hitherto it has been given."

Leif J. Braaten and C. Douglas Darling, "Overt and Covert Homosexual Problems Among Male College Students," *Genetic Psychology Monographs*, 71 (1965): 302–03.

- Daniel G. Brown reported that when he served as a psychiatrist in the U.S. Air Force, "there was the opportunity to interview and test approximately 40 male airmen in whom predominant or exclusive homosexuality was the major problem. In more than 30 of these cases, the mother-son and father-son relationship conformed to the family pattern described above. Not one of these airmen had a close, warm, affectionate attachment to his father or a father-substitute in childhood."

Daniel G. Brown, "Homosexuality and Family Dynamics," *Bulletin of the Menninger Clinic* 27 (5): 229 (Sept. 1963).

Evelyn Hooker questions Bieber's findings

UCLA professor Evelyn Hooker was the author of numerous studies that purported to show that homosexuality does not involve pathology. Hooker criticized Bieber's work because it involved subjects who were undergoing psychiatric treatment and thus the results are presumably not applicable to the broader population of homosexuals. Hooker, who has been accused of introducing methodological errors and bias into her own work, claimed:

- "The etiological role of parental relationships in producing homosexuality is an *inference* which cannot be justified from psychiatric samples alone, in part because of the contamination of homosexuality with psychopathology."

Evelyn Hooker, "Parental Relations and Male Homosexuality in Patient and Nonpatient Samples," *Journal of Consulting and Clinical Psychology*, 33 (April 1969): 140.

Reply to Hooker's criticism

What Hooker failed to acknowledge was that the study of research subjects under medical evaluation and treatment is a widely-used and valid research method. In addition, Hooker herself has been criticized for recruiting research subjects from radical homosexual groups and others with an obvious agenda to promote (see Thomas Landess, "The Evelyn Hooker Study and the Normalization of Homosexuality," [Family Research Council, 1995]).

Meanwhile, other research drawn from subjects in the general population confirmed the work of Bieber and others.

The contribution of Ray B. Evans

In 1969 a study by Ray B. Evans of the Loma Linda University School of Medicine was published in the *Journal of Consulting and Clinical Psychology*. It addressed Hooker's criticism and supported Bieber's findings of greater family dysfunction in the childhood of homosexuals.

- Whereas Bieber's data was "based on psychoanalysts' reconstructions of patients' early life circumstances, derived from impressions during psychotherapy ... in the present study, the data were based on retrospective self-reports of how they now view their childhood, by (study subjects) who had never been in psychotherapy." Study author Ray B. Evans of the Loma Linda University School of Medicine concluded: "The present results were remarkably similar to those of Bieber et al. in revealing more 'negative' features in the backgrounds of homosexuals."

  Ray B. Evans, "Childhood Parental Relationships of Homosexual Men," *Journal of Counseling and Clinical Psychology*, 33 (April 1969): 129, 133.

- Describing his findings in more detail, Evans reports that the mothers of homosexuals "more often were considered puritanical, cold toward men, insisted on being the center of the son's attention, made him her confidant, were 'seductive' toward him, allied with him against the father, openly preferred him to the father, interfered with his heterosexual activities during adolescence, discouraged masculine attitudes and encouraged feminine ones. The fathers of the homosexuals were retrospectively considered as less likely to encourage masculine attitudes and activities, and (the study subjects) spent little time with their fathers, were more often aware of hating him and afraid he might physically harm them, less often were the

23

father's favorite, felt less accepted by him, and in turn less frequently accepted or respected the father....The results strongly suggested poor parental relationships during childhood for the homosexual men, at least as seen in retrospect."

Evans, "Childhood Parental Relationships of Homosexual Men," 133.

Was Evans too cautious regarding his conclusions?

- Evans concluded his article with a note of caution as to whether his findings show that poor parental relationships cause homosexuality: "The results of the present study agreed closely with those obtained by Bieber et al.. but they neither supported nor refuted the Bieber conclusions as to causal relationships."

Evans, "Childhood Parental Relationships of Homosexual Men," 135.

However, two other scholars, asked to comment on Evans' article in the same issue of *Journal of Consulting and Clinical Psychology*, said that his caution was unwarranted:

- The first, Ralph H. Gundlach, flatly stated that "Evans' argument, that an association between questionnaire items regarding parent-to-child behaviors and later homosexuality is not causal, is rejected as not applicable."

Gundlach, "Childhood Parental Relationships and the Establishment of Gender Roles of Homosexuals," 136.

- The second response came from none other than Evelyn Hooker: "Evans' study is therefore of special importance as a partial confirmation of the Bieber assumption about causal relation between parental relations in early childhood and adult homosexuality. In my view, Evans is overly cautious in his assertion that his findings neither confirm nor refute the etiological role of parent-child relations as one set of many variables influencing or causing homosexuality in adult life. Indeed, his study necessitates this generalization since it is a replication."

Hooker, "Parental Relations and Male Homosexuality in Patient and Nonpatient Samples," 140-41.

Hooker v. Hooker

We find in Hooker's writings other admissions that seem at odds with her overall viewpoint.

- While admitting that while studies such as Evans were a "partial confirmation" of Bieber, she insisted they were "not conclusive." Nonetheless, she acknowledged the validity of studies that do not utilize patients who are undergoing therapy: "Similar results with nonpatient samples tend to confirm ... the etiological role of parental relationships in producing homosexuality."

- In fact, Hooker herself mentions several studies that control for the presence of unrelated psychopathology: "In the Schofield (1965) study, homosexual men in a nonpatient sample reported a higher incidence of poor relations with the father and of overprotective or overpossessive mothers than did a similar sample of heterosexual men."

Hooker, "Parental Relations and Male Homosexuality in Patient and Nonpatient Samples," 140.

Other confirmations of Bieber's findings

- A 1969 study was published in *Psychological Reports* that was designed to address criticisms such as raised by Hooker. Authors John R. Snortum, et al., incorporated a non-patient control group: "In this study, then, the investigators, the methods, and (subjects) were drawn from outside of the circle of psychoanalytic study." The authors concluded that "the present findings lend strong support to the earlier results obtained by Bieber, *et al.* (1962)," including the formative influence of "the pathological interplay between a close-binding, controlling mother and a rejecting and detached father."

John R. Snortum, James F. Gillespie, John E. Marshall, John P. McLaughlin, and Ludwig Mosberg, "Family Dynamics and Homosexuality," *Psychological Reports*, 24 (1969): 763.

- A 1974 study comparing 307 homosexuals with a control group of 138 heterosexuals, both from nonclinical samples, confirmed Bieber, et al.: "The homosexuals, in contrast to the heterosexuals, reported their fathers to be more rejecting and less loving. The homosexuals also described their mothers as more rejecting and less loving…the homosexuals indicated less closeness to their fathers than the hetero-sexuals."

Marvin Siegelman, "Parental Background of Male Homosexuals and Heterosexuals," *Archives of Sexual Behavior*, 3 (1974): 10 .

- Others studies could be cited, as they were by Siegelman: "Sup-port for the 'triangular system' hypothesis has been presented by Benda (1963), Braatan and Darling (1965), Brown (1963), Edwards (1963), Evans (1969), Jonas (1944), O'Connor (1964), Snortum et al. (1969), and Whitener and Nikelly (1964)."

Ibid., 3 (1): 3-4 (1974).

- Even three decades of research later, the *Archives of General Psychiatry* found that "the literature suggests that many, perhaps a majority, of homosexual men report family constellations similar to those sug-gested by Bieber et al. to be causally associated with the development of homosexuality (e.g., overly involved, anxiously overcontrolling mothers, poor father-son relationships). This association has been observed in nonclinical as well as clinical samples."

Byne and Parsons, "Human Sexual Orientation: The Biologic Theories Reappraised," 236.

Summary of findings regarding the developmental causes of homosexuality

Daniel G. Brown put it well forty years ago—but his ringing call to action has gone unheeded for the past thirty years:

- "In summary, then, it would seem that the family pattern involving a combination of a dominating, overly intimate mother *plus* a detached, hostile or weak father is beyond doubt related to the development of male homosexuality. Beginning with the penetrating clinical insights of Freud 50 years ago, the systematic investigation by Terman and Miles some 30 years ago, the independent findings of a number of clinical and research workers, and the recent noteworthy contributions of West and Bieber, there is now strong evidence and considerable agreement as to family dynamics in the development of male homosexuality. It is surprising there has not been greater rec-ognition of this relationship among the various disciplines that are concerned with children. A problem that arises in this connection is how to inform and educate teachers and parents relative to the decisive influence of the family in determining the course and outcome of the child's psychosexual development. There would seem to be no justification for waiting another 25 or 50 years to bring this information to the attention of those who deal with children. And there is no excuse for professional workers in the behavioral sciences to continue avoiding their responsibility to disseminate this knowledge and understanding as widely as possible."

Daniel G. Brown, "Homosexuality and Family Dynamics," *Bulletin of the Menninger Clinic* 27 (5): 232 (Sept. 1963).

The "exotic becomes erotic" theory

Another more recent theory regarding the development of same-sex attraction is offered by Daryl Bem of Cornell University.

- Bem's "Exotic Becomes Erotic" theory of erotic/romantic attraction held that "biological variables, such as genes, prenatal hormones, and brain neuroanatomy, do not code for sexual orientation per se but for childhood temperaments that influence a child's preferences for sex-typical or sex-atypical activities and peers. These preferences lead children to feel different from opposite or same-sex peers—to perceive them as dissimilar, unfamiliar, and exotic. This, in turn, produces heightened nonspecific autonomic arousal that subsequently gets eroticized to that same class of dissimilar peers: Exotic becomes erotic…The theory claims to accommodate both the empirical evidence of the biological essentialists and the cultural relativism of the social constructionists."

- Bem's theory suggests that a child's experience of being "different" from peers of the same gender leads to a reaction of physical arousal, which then later in life becomes translated into sexual arousal—a process he calls 'sexual imprinting.' Bem mentions the illustration of a "gender-nonconforming boy who is taunted by other boys. At first this produces strong negative arousal, but with repeated encounters over time, the fear and anger habituate and the opponent process becomes the conditioned, dominant affect. He thus emerges into late childhood or adolescence experiencing positive affective arousal to males, an arousal ready to be eroticized."

Bem, "Exotic Becomes Erotic: A Developmental Theory of Sexual Orientation," *Psychological Review*, 103 (1966): 327.

- In a similar vein, psychiatrists Byne and Parsons propose an "interactional model," in which genes or hormones do not specify sexual orientation per se, but instead bias particular personality traits and thereby influence the manner in which an individual and his or her environment interacts as sexual orientation and other personality characteristics unfold developmentally. Such a mechanism would allow for multiple developmental pathways leading to homosexuality and would account for the high concordance rate for homosexuality among identical twins reared together, as well as for the failures of various psychosocial theories that have focused exclusively either on personality traits of individuals or on various environmental factors, but not on the interaction of the two."

Byne and Parsons, "Human Sexual Orientation: The Biologic Theories Reappraised," 236–37.

Child Sexual Abuse and the Development of Homosexuality

A study in the *Journal of Sex & Marital Therapy* examined the past sexual experiences, sexual thoughts, and fantasies regarding the sexual contacts of 35 adult men who were sexually abused during their childhoods. The study found that among men, a history of homosexual child abuse was linked both to an adult homosexual orientation and to sexual attraction to children:

- "According to existing literature, gender identity confusion and gender preference are often cited as being affected by childhood sexual abuse. In this study, 46 percent of the abused men, as opposed to 12 percent of the nonabused men, defined their sexual orientation as either bisexual or homosexual. Therefore, these findings further validate previous research regarding the sexual orientation of children who have been sexually abused."

- The study concludes: "Given these findings, it appears that being sexually abused as a child may affect the propensity of adult men to fantasize about young men."

James R. Bramblett, Jr., and Carol Anderson Darling, "Sexual Contacts: Experiences, Thoughts, and Fantasies of Adult Male Survivors of Child Sexual Abuse," *Journal of Sex & Marital Therapy*, 23 (4): 313 (Winter 1997).

- The *Bulletin of the Menninger Clinic* mentions "seduction" among a list of other possible childhood experiences that could contribute to same-sex attraction: "There are a number of factors that occur in childhood which appear to be related to the development of homosexuality in adults. Such conditions as prolonged segregation of the sexes; specific, intensely exciting, and gratifying homosexual experiences in childhood; seduction by adult homosexuals; threatening and painful experiences in connection with sex play or relationships with the opposite sex; these and related factors in childhood and adolescence are correlated with the occurrence of homosexuality in adulthood."

Brown, "Homosexuality and Family Dynamics," 228.

Cultural Factors in the Development of Homosexuality

If homosexuality were a result of biological or genetic factors, one might expect that it would be fairly evenly distributed both geographically and sociologically among all types of people. However, the research into Americans' sexual behavior and self-identification by sexual orientation indicates that this is not the case. Two factors, in particular, stand out as having a strong correlation with a greater likelihood of engaging in homosexual acts or self-identifying as homosexual: urbanization and education.

Urbanization

Homosexuals tend to be concentrated in urban areas:

- The National Health and Social Life Survey found that homosexuals and lesbians are not evenly distributed across the country. Rather, "more than 9 percent of the men in the nation's twelve largest cities identify themselves as gay. But just 3 or 4 percent of men living in the suburbs of these cities or in most of the larger cities of the nation say they are gay, and about 1 percent of men in rural areas identify themselves as gay. Lesbians, too, cluster in cities, but the tendency is not so pronounced as for gay men."

  Robert T. Michael, John H. Gagnon, Edward O. Laumann, and Gina Kolata, *Sex in America: A Definitive Survey* (Boston: Little, Brown and Co., 1994), 177–79.

- *The Social Organization of Sexuality* gives additional details on the "striking" relationship between "the level of urbanization of the current residence of respondents and the various measures of same-gender sexuality. Men living in the central cities of the twelve largest metropolitan areas reports rates of same-gender sexuality of between 9.2 and 16.7 percent (…referring to *identity* and *desire*, respectively), a compared to rates for all men on these measures of 2.8 and 7.7 percent, respectively. And the rates generally decline monotonically with decline in urbanization. While the rates of reported same-gender sexuality for women generally follow a similar pattern to those for men, that is, they are positively correlated with degree of urbanization, this pattern is not nearly so marked as with the men."

Laumann, et al., *The Social Organization of Sexuality*, 306.

Chart 1: Percentage with any same-gender sexual contact since puberty, by place of residence

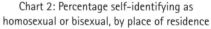

- 12 largest central cities
- Suburbs of 12 largest central cities
- Next 88 central cities
- Suburbs of next 88 central cities
- Other urban areas
- Rural areas

Chart 2: Percentage self-identifying as homosexual or bisexual, by place of residence

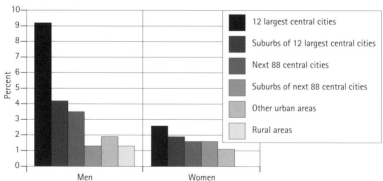

- 12 largest central cities
- Suburbs of 12 largest central cities
- Next 88 central cities
- Suburbs of next 88 central cities
- Other urban areas
- Rural areas

Source: Edward O. Laumann, John H. Gagnon, Robert T. Michael, and Stuart Michaels, *The Social Organization of Sexuality: Sexual Practices in the United States* (Chicago: The University of Chicago Press, 1994), Table 8.2, 305.

- The *Demography* study elaborates on the high levels urbanization among homosexuals: "The 20 cities with large numbers of gay couples, which are home to less than 26 percent of the U.S. population, contain nearly 60 percent of our sample of gay men. Clearly gay men are concentrated in a selected number of urban areas. Lesbian women are somewhat less geographically concentrated....some cities have atypically high concentrations of gays and lesbians. For example, a randomly selected gay man in our sample is about 12 times more likely to live in San Francisco than are other individuals in the U.S. population. Other cities with especially high concentrations of gays include Los Angeles, Washington, DC, and Atlanta. High concentrations of lesbian women are found in San Francisco, Seattle, and Minneapolis. When we look at concentrations of gay and lesbian couples in smaller cities (e.g., 200,000 to 700,000), we find a disproportionate number of 'college towns' such as Ann Arbor and Madison. (For both gays and lesbians, seven of the 10 smaller cities with high concentrations contain a major university.)"

Black, et al., "Demographics of the Gay and Lesbian Population in the United States," 148–49.

- Of course, one possible explanation for such a finding could be that homosexuals are more evenly spread across the country at birth, but tend to gravitate in adulthood toward larger cities where they can find greater acceptance and a substantial community of other homosexuals. However, Michael et al. question this interpretation, pointing out that "it is not just that homosexuals tend to move to large cities from the small towns and rural areas where they grew up." Instead, they cite findings that "people who were raised in large cities were more likely to be homosexual than people who were raised in suburbs, towns, or the countryside. This relationship also showed up in the General Social Survey, an independent national sample."

Robert T. Michael, John H. Gagnon, Edward O. Laumann, and Gina Kolata, *Sex in America: A Definitive Survey* (Boston: Little, Brown and Co., 1994), 182.

- Michael et al. directly contradict the notion that people are "born gay" with their hypothesis on why an urban upbringing is correlated with homosexuality: "It might be that it is easier for a person to be gay to learn to be gay or to explore a gay lifestyle growing up in a larger community that has other gays."

Michael, et al., *Sex in America*, 182.

• A more detailed explanation of how a social environment that affirms a homosexual identity and behavior can increase the prevalence of homosexuality was described decades ago in the *British Journal of Psychiatry*: "If he frequents certain inns and other haunts where homosexuals foregather, he is encouraged to practice homosexuality; frequent indulgence may remove the anxiety about failing to mature and at the same time satisfy the sexual drive. The mutual support given by the rest of the coterie encourages the homosexual to believe he is one of a race apart without hope of cure and therefore entitled to indulge in his now firmly established homosexual habits....If the outlook is hopeless and cure is impossible, the subject argues that he is entitled to indulge his sexual drive in the only way he can and that society must accept his homosexuality."

P. J. O'Connor, "Aetiological Factors in Homosexuality as Seen in Royal Air Force Psychiatric Practice," *British Journal of Psychiatry*, 466: 386 (May 1964).

Education

As with urbanization, higher levels of education are directly correlated with higher levels of homosexual behavior and self-identification.

• A study in the journal *Science* found, "Men with four or more years of college are estimated to have a higher proportion" with same-gender sexual experience, "particularly compared to those with no college education."

Robert E. Fay, Charles F. Turner, Albert D. Klassen, John H. Gagnon, "Prevalence and Patterns of Same-Gender Sexual Contact Among Men," *Science* 243, Issue 4889 (20 January 1989): 342.

• Another study of men, published in *Family Planning Perspectives*, found that education was "positively associated with having had a same-gender sexual experience within the last ten years...."

John O. G. Billy, Koray Tanfer, William R. Grady and Daniel H. Klepinger, "The Sexual Behavior of Men In the United States," *Family Planning Perspectives* 25, no. 2 (March/April 1993): 59.

• The comprehensive National Health and Social Life Survey (NHSLS) reached the same conclusion: "Our study shows that twice as many college-educated men identify themselves as homosexual as men with high-school educations, 3 percent of college-educated men said they were gay compared to 1.5 percent of men with high-school educations."

Robert T. Michael, John H. Gagnon, Edward O. Laumann, and Gina Kolata, *Sex in America: A Definitive Survey* (Boston: Little, Brown and Co., 1994), 182.

- However, the authors of *Sex in America* reported, "For women the trend is even more striking. Women with college educations are eight times more likely to identify themselves as lesbians as are women with a high-school education. Four percent of female college graduates identify themselves as lesbians as compared to less than half a percent of female high-school graduates."

Michael et al., *Sex in America: A Definitive Survey*, 182.

Chart 1: Percentage with any same-gender sexual contact since puberty, by level of education

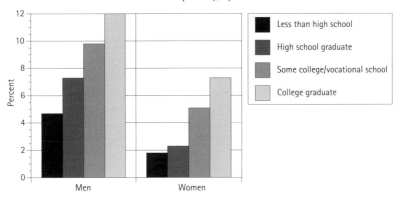

Chart 2: Percentage self-identifying as homosexual or bisexual, by level of education

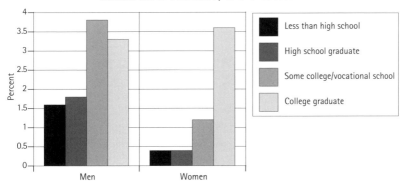

Source: Edward O. Laumann, John H. Gagnon, Robert T. Michael, and Stuart Michaels, *The Social Organization of Sexuality: Sexual Practices in the United States* (Chicago: The University of Chicago Press, 1994), Table 8.2, 305

- Again, the interpretation offered in the most scholarly treatment of the NHSLS data, *The Social Organization of Sexuality*," supports the notion that the ideological environment rather than any innate characteristic accounts for this finding: "Higher levels of education are associated with greater social and sexual liberalism" and with "greater sexual experimentation." Laumann et al. conclude, "Acceptance of nontraditional sexual behavior is likely to be higher among the more educated."

Edward O. Laumann, John H. Gagnon, Robert T. Michael, and Stuart Michaels, *The Social Organization of Sexuality: Sexual Practices in the United States* (Chicago: The University of Chicago Press, 1994), 309.

The Role of Personal Choice in Becoming Homosexual

Debates over homosexuality are often presented in terms of a false dichotomy—either a person is "born gay," or a person "chooses to be gay." The truth lies between these two extremes. For the most part, people do not choose what sexual feelings or attractions they experience. Each of us does, however, choose the sexual behaviors in which we engage:

- Writing with reference to lesbians, Bem notes that "some women who would otherwise be predicted by the EBE model to have a heterosexual orientation might choose for social or political reasons to center their lives around other women. This could lead them to avoid seeking out men for sexual or romantic relationships, to develop affectional and erotic ties to other women, and to self-identify as lesbians or bisexuals."

Bem, "Exotic Becomes Erotic: A Developmental Theory of Sexual Orientation," 331.

- Writing in *Archives of General Psychiatry* Byne and Parsons note the role that "choice" plays in the development of one's "sexual orientation": "Conspicuously absent from most theorizing on the origins of sexual orientation is an active role of the individual in constructing his or her identity." The authors explain: "This is not meant to imply that one consciously decides one's sexual orientation. Instead, sexual orientation is assumed to be shaped and reshaped by a cascade of choices made in the context of changing circumstances in one's life and enormous social and cultural pressures."

Byne and Parsons, "Human Sexual Orientation: The Biologic Theories Reappraised," 236–237.

34

CHAPTER 2

How Many Homosexuals Are There?

One of the most fundamental questions regarding homosexuals in America—the question of how many of them there are—has been the subject of dispute. It is our view that this is one of the questions about which misinformation and misunderstanding is most widespread. Those who advocate greater acceptance of homosexuality have often done so, in part, by arguing that homosexual behavior is relatively common.

The estimate most often cited is that "10 percent" of the population is homosexual.

- Such a figure would make the number of homosexuals comparable to the numbers in prominent ethnic minority groups such as African Americans (12.3 percent, according to the 2000 census) or Hispanics (13 percent).

  William G. Barron, acting director, U. S. Census Bureau, Dept. of Commerce, "Census 2000: The Results Start Rolling In," in *The World Almanac and Book of Facts 2002* (New York: World Almanac Education Group, Inc., 2002), 374.

We believe that the "10 percent" figure is grossly exaggerated. Let's see what the research shows.

A note on sources

One of the most valuable sources of information regarding the sexual behavior and identity of the American people is the National Health and Social Life Survey (NHSLS). Designed by scholars at the University of Chicago and conducted by the National Opinion Research Center (NORC), the NHSLS was a survey in 1992 of over 3,000 Americans. The results were published in

1994 in two separate volumes, one more scholarly and one written at a more popular level. The scholarly version was:

Edward O. Laumann, John H. Gagnon, Robert T. Michael, and Stuart Michaels, *The Social Organization of Sexuality: Sexual Practices in the United States* (Chicago: The University of Chicago Press, 1994).

The more popular version was:

Robert T. Michael, John H. Gagnon, Edward O. Laumann, and Gina Kolata, *Sex in America: A Definitive Survey* (Boston: Little, Brown and Co., 1994).

Both works are cited at various times in this chapter, but the reader should be aware that both are describing the same data set. Because of this, and because the authors of both works are mostly the same, we have sometimes cited these works by title rather than by author.

Is "10 Percent" of the Population Homosexual?

The oft-repeated assertion that "10 percent" of the population is homosexual has been promoted by homosexual activists:

- Edward O. Laumann, et al., writing in *The Social Organization of Sexuality: Sexual Practices in the United States*, report that this claim has been used by homosexual activists to promote gay rights: "In fact, Bruce Voeller (1990) claims to have originated the 10 percent estimate as part of the modern gay-rights movement's campaign in the late 1970s to convince politicians and the public that 'We [gays and lesbians] Are Everywhere.' At the time, Voeller was the chair of the National Gay Task Force."

  Edward O. Laumann, John H. Gagnon, Robert T. Michael, and Stuart Michaels, *The Social Organization of Sexuality: Sexual Practices in the United States* (Chicago: The University of Chicago Press, 1994), 289, footnote 7; citing Bruce Voeller, "Some Uses and Abuses of the Kinsey Scale," in *Homosexuality-Heterosexuality: Concepts of Sexual Orientation*, ed. David P. McWhirter, Stephanie A. Saunders and June Machover Reinisch (New York: Oxford University Press, 1990).

- Homosexual activist Bruce Voeller has also written that "after years of our educating those who inform the public and make its laws, the concept that 10 percent of the population is gay has become a generally accepted 'fact.' While some reminding always seems necessary, the 10 percent figure is regularly utilized by scholars, by the press, and in government statistics. As with so many other pieces of knowledge (and myth), repeated telling made it so..."

  Voeller, "Some Uses and Abuses of the Kinsey Scale," 33–36.

- The "myth" of the 10 percent figure was uncritically accepted by many, as reported by *Newsweek*: "For years, the gay-rights movement has sought safety in numbers. Its leaders have long claimed that homosexuals constitute 10 percent of the American population. They cited Alfred Kinsey, who interviewed thousands of men and women for landmark studies on human sexuality in the 1940s and 1950s....Policymakers and the press (including *Newsweek*) adopted the estimate—despite protests from skeptical conservatives—citing it time and again."

  Patrick Rogers, "How Many Gays Are There?" *Newsweek* 15 (February 1993): 46.

The origin of the "10 percent" claim

The 10 percent claim is said to have originated from the infamous Indiana University sex researcher Alfred Kinsey (d. 1956). However, Kinsey's methodology has been challenged as unscientific and unreliable.

- An analysis of Kinsey's data by Milton Diamond in *Archives of Sexual Behavior* finds that his interview subjects were unrepresentative of the U.S. population as a whole. According to Diamond, Kinsey's fellow researchers admitted to him that "the original Kinsey studies had many respondents associated with known gay groups. This too biased their sample. None of the randomized studies indicated they culled their samples of individuals of known gay organizations nor of those with histories of incarceration."

  Milton Diamond, Ph.D., "Homosexuality and Bisexuality in Different Populations," *Archives of Sexual Behavior* 22 (1993): 298–99.

- The book *Sex in America* puts it this way: "Kinsey almost certainly included people who were more sexually active and more willing to discuss their sex lives. He also made it more likely that he would find homosexuals by recruiting volunteers in prisons and reform schools and by asking homosexuals who were part of social networks in large cities to bring in their friends and acquaintances to be part of his study."

  Robert T. Michael, et al., "Sex in America," 174.

- *The Social Organization of Sexuality* elaborates, saying of Kinsey's sampling techniques, "These devices would all tend to bias Kinsey's results toward higher estimates of homosexuality (and other rarer sexual practices) than those that he would have obtained using probability sampling." It notes that "there is no statistically sound way to generalize from his sample to a population." As a result, "Kinsey's figures are much higher than those found in all the recent population surveys, including ours."

Edward O. Laumann, et al., "The Social Organization of Sexuality," 289.

- An article in the journal *Science* declared, "Even 40 years ago, Kinsey's data were regarded as unsuitable" for making estimates "of the size of the population of men who have sex with men." It added, "Since the Kinsey sample was not a probability sample, the data do not allow estimation of the characteristics of the national populations with knowable margins of error. It is this point that is made most trenchantly in the major statistical reviews of Kinsey's research."

Robert E. Fay, Charles F. Turner, Albert D. Klassen, John H. Gagnon, "Prevalence and Patterns of Same-Gender Sexual Contact Among Men," *Science* 243, Issue 4889 (20 January 1989): 338.

- Even homosexual advocacy research publications have questioned Kinsey's methodology. The *Journal of Homosexuality* points out, "Although people often use Kinsey's research to assert that approximately 10 percent of the population is gay, researchers have noted that there are several problems with this statistic. First, Kinsey did not use probability sampling methods to construct his sample of the population. Therefore, it is fallacious to generalize from his biased sample to the larger society....[T]he 10 percent estimate provided in Kinsey's study of men is derived from Kinsey's study of white men and does not, therefore, address the question of homosexuality (however defined) among women and minorities."

Matthew V. Pruitt, "Size Matters: A Comparison of Anti- and Pro-Gay Organizations' Estimates of the Size of the Gay Population," *Journal of Homosexuality* 42 (2002):22.

- The *Gay and Lesbian Review Worldwide* reiterates the weaknesses of the Kinsey research: "Most people have concluded that 10 percent is probably an overestimate. The major criticism is that Kinsey's sample was skewed to over-sample for the homosexually inclined—for example, it included a large number of male prisoners."

Richard Schneider, Jr., "'The People Gay' and the 10 Percent Debate," *Gay and Lesbian Review Worldwide* 7(2): 4–6 (Spring 2000), Academic Search Premier AN 2990702, ISSN 1532-1118.

- The final word on the "10 percent" estimate may be summarized in a *Newsweek* report on the issue: "The 10 percent—which represents adult males who said they were predominantly homosexual for at least three years—suggests that a significant part of Kinsey's sample was gay, but nothing more. 'It's just not a real number,' says University of Washington sociologist Pepper Schwartz."

Rogers, "How Many Gays Are There?" 46.

Kinsey did not claim that 10 percent of the population is homosexual

It is worth pointing out that even with his skewed research, Kinsey did not conclude that 10 percent of Americans are homosexual.

- The *Gay and Lesbian Review Worldwide* admits that "Kinsey's '10 percent' category was defined very broadly, and certainly included lots of people who wouldn't qualify as out gay men or lesbians by today's definition."

  Richard Schneider, Jr., "'The People Gay' and the 10 Percent Debate," *Gay and Lesbian Review Worldwide* 7 (Spring 2000), Academic Search Premier AN 2990702, ISSN 1532-1118.

- Michael, et al., elaborate, stating that Kinsey's "10 percent" figure was limited to those who claimed to have "had only homosexual experiences for any three-year period between ages sixteen and fifty-five (this is probably where the popularized 10 percent figure came from)....In fact, a reanalysis of the Kinsey data for college men only, showed that the proportion of men who said they had had exclusively homosexual experiences since age eighteen was 3 percent..."

  John H. Gagnon and William Simon, *Sexual Conduct* (Chicago: Aldine Press, 1973), cited in Michael, et al., *Sex in America*, 173.

Recent research does not support the "10 percent" claim

- *Newsweek* reports that "new evidence suggests that ideology, not sound science, has perpetuated a 1-in-10 myth. In the nearly half century since Kinsey, no survey has come close to duplicating his findings."

  Patrick Rogers, "How Many Gays Are There?" *Newsweek* 15 (February 1993): 46.

- A review of studies from the U.S. and abroad published in the *Archives of Sexual Behavior* concludes: "No study finds any figure reaching 10 percent for all respondents experiences with homosexual and bisexual activity combined....All these studies taken together indicate that bisexuality, and indeed homosexuality, are less common than previously considered."

Diamond, "Homosexuality in Different Populations," 303.

- The review recommends that "the oft-used 10 percent figure needs downward revision in light of the more reliable and valid data from the scientifically randomized samples reported here."

Ibid., 305.

- Laumann, et al., concur: "[A]ll the recent population-based surveys of sexual behavior, including this one, have found rates that are much lower than 10 percent."

Laumann, et al., *The Social Organization of Sexuality*, 286.

The political agenda behind promoting the 10 percent figure

A study in the homosexual advocacy research publication *Journal of Homosexuality* outline the reasons for promoting the 10 percent figure:

- "First, the size of the gay population has potential political ramifications....More gay people, quite straightforwardly, means more political clout....For politicians of either ilk ["pro-gay" or "anti-gay"] the size of the gay vote is an important political factor....Second, business and corporate decisions may be directly or indirectly influenced by estimates of the size of the gay community. For example, corporations have advertised in gay magazines, provided gay-pride color beer lights to gay bars, and shown same-sex couples in advertisements (e.g., IKEA, Bud Light)...Third, many gay groups actively seek to make the transition to self-acceptance easier for those people who are coming to terms with the fact that they have a same-sex sexual orientation....The message that most clearly links to the size of the gay population is 'You are not alone.' Clearly, one is less alone is 10 percent of the population is gay than if 1–3 percent of the population is gay."

Matthew V. Pruitt, "Size Matters," 26–27.

- Michael, et al., agree: "Many gay groups would like the number to be large, so they can argue that homosexuals are a force to be reckoned with, that any politician who avoids or alienates gay voters does so at his or her peril. They have promoted the phrase "one in ten"—one American in ten is gay or lesbian, they assert."

Robert T. Michael, John H. Gagnon, Edward O. Laumann, and Gina Kolata, *Sex in America: A Definitive Survey* (Boston: Little, Brown and Co., 1994), 172.

What Percentage of the Population is Homosexual?

The difficulty of claiming that a certain percentage of the population is unalterably "gay" is explained in the book *Sex in America*:

- "First, people often change their sexual behavior during their life-times, making it impossible to state that a particular set of behaviors defines a person as gay....Often implicit in a [single fixed] figure...is the assumption that homosexuality is a characteristic like green eyes that is part of a person's identity and never changes."

- "A second reason is that there is no one set of sexual desires or self-identification that uniquely defines homosexuality. Is it sexual desire for a person of the same gender, it is thinking of yourself as a homosexual, or is it some combination of these behaviors that makes a person a homosexual?"

- "A third reason is that homosexual behavior is not easily measured."

Michael, et al., *Sex in America*, 172

- The *Social Organization of Sexuality* notes that "homosexuality is a complex, multidimensional phenomenon whose salient features are related to one another in highly contingent and diverse ways."

Laumann, et al., *The Social Organization of Sexuality*, 320.

- Similarly, Diamond asks: "Would individuals who had 1 or 2 homo-sexual experiences and 100 heterosexual ones be rated the same as someone who had had 1 and 10?...Do we include or exclude adolescent experimentation or prison experiences that are never repeated? How should one distinguish between self-identifica-tion and labeling by professionals? Should we reserve the terms 'homosexual,' 'bisexual,' or 'heterosexual' for an individual's activities or fantasies or both…?"

Diamond, "Homosexuality and Bisexuality in Different Populations," 297.

Measuring the Homosexual Population

Laumann, et al., describe how homosexuality is measured: "For the purpose of this analysis, we have divided the questions that relate to homosexual experiences and feelings into three basic dimensions: behavior, desire, and identity."

Laumann, et al., *The Social Organization of Sexuality*, 292–93.

The homosexual population measured by "self-reporting" or "identity"

One means of ascertaining the percentage of homosexuals in a population is by counting those who describe themselves as homosexual. According to this measure, homosexuals comprise a very low percentage of the population:

- *Sex in America: A Definitive Survey* reports: "We asked respondents whether they consider themselves heterosexual, homosexual, bisexual, or something else. This question elicited the lowest rates of homosexuality. About 1.4 percent of the women said they thought of themselves as homosexual or bisexual and about 2.8 percent of the men identified themselves in this way.…No matter how we define homosexuality, we come up with small percentages of people who are currently gay or lesbian."

  Michael, et al., *Sex in America*, 176–77.

- Even the leading homosexual activist groups in the country conceded the validity of these same estimates, in a little-noticed footnote to the brief they submitted to the U.S. Supreme Court in the *Lawrence v. Texas* sodomy case in 2003: "The most widely accepted study of sexual practices in the United States is the National Health and Social Life Survey (NHSLS). The NHSLS found that 2.8 percent of the male, and 1.4 percent of the female, population identify themselves as gay, lesbian, or bisexual. See Laumann et al.,

The Social Organization of Sex: Sexual Practices in the United States (1994)."

Lawrence v. Texas, Docket No. 02-102 (U.S. Supreme Court), brief of amici curiae Human Rights Campaign et al., 16 January 2003, 16 (footnote 42).

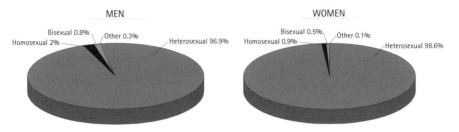

Chart: Sexual Orientation of Americans (by Self-Identification)

Source: Edward O. Laumann, John H. Gagnon, Robert T. Michael, and Stuart Michaels, *The Social Organization of Sexuality: Sexual Practices in the United States* (Chicago: The University of Chicago Press, 1994), 311, Table 8.3B.

The percentage of young people self-identifying as homosexual

- A study in *Pediatrics* of 4,159 high school students in Massachusetts found similarly low percentages of youth who self-identify as homosexual: "Sexual orientation was determined by the following question: 'Which of the following best describes you?' A total of 104 students self-identified as gay, lesbian, or bisexual (GLB), representing 2.5 percent of the overall population. Of GLB youth, 66.7 percent were male..."

Robert Garofalo, MD; R. Cameron Wolf, MS; Shari Kessel, ScB; Judith Palfrey, MD; and Robert H. DuRant, PhD; "The Association Between Health Risk Behaviors and Sexual Orientation Among a School-based Sample of Adolescents," *Pediatrics* 101 (May 1998): 895–902.

The homosexual population measured by behavior

The percentage of youths who actually engage in homosexual behavior:

- *Family Planning Perspectives* analyzed the National Longitudinal Study of Adolescent Health, which surveyed 18,924 adolescents from 132 schools and found an extremely low level of homosexual behavior. The report said, "The final data set for our analysis included 17,266 heterosexual relationships, which were reported by 8,024 adolescents." By comparison, the survey respondents "reported only 20 homosexual relationships. These relationships were removed from the data file because they were two few to include in our analyses." This means that 0.1 percent—about one in a thousand—of the adolescent "sexual relationships" identified by the researchers were homosexual in nature.

Kathleen Ford, Woosung Sohn, and James Lepkowski, "Characteristics of Adolescents' Sexual Partners and Their Association with Use of Condoms and Other Contraceptive Methods," *Family Planning Perspectives* 33 (May/June 2001): 101.

With regard to the population as a whole, researchers have used various measures to ascertain the percentages of those who have engaged in homosexual activity, including:

Those engaging in homosexual behavior during the previous year:

- The *Archives of Sexual Behavior* study reports a 1988 National Opinion Research Center (NORC) random household study, which found that "only 2.4 percent of their males indicated same-sex behavior within the preceding year." A 1991 NORC study "found less than 2 percent of sexually active adult males and females… reported exclusive homosexual or bisexual activity the preceding year. After adjusting for 'uncertain' or nonresponding cases Smith reported only 0.7 percent were exclusively homosexual since the age of 18…"

  Diamond, "Homosexuality and Bisexuality in Different Populations," 299.

- In measuring homosexual behavior, Laumann, et al., conclude: "The rates for women are lower than the rates for men, varying from 1.3 percent of the sexually active women in the past year reporting at least one female partner to 4.1 percent reporting any female partners since turning eighteen. The rates for men vary from 2.7 percent in the past year to 4.9 percent with any male partners since age eighteen."

  Laumann, et al., *The Social Organization of Sexuality*, 294.

During the previous 10 years:

- A nationally representative study of the sexual behavior of men aged

20–39 reported in *Family Planning Perspectives* found that only 2.3 percent of "sexually active men aged 20–39 have had any same-gender sexual activity during the last 10 years, and only 1 percent reported being exclusively homosexual during this interval."

John O. G. Billy, Koray Tanfer, William R. Grady and Daniel H. Klepinger, "The Sexual Behavior of Men in the United States," *Family Planning Perspectives* 25 (March/April 1993): 52, 59.

Since puberty:

- The *Archives of Sexual Behavior* reported, "If we use the largest figures available…within each study, we find a mean of 5.5 percent and a median of 5.3 percent represents the population of males having engaged in same-sex behavior. Female figures are even smaller: mean 2.5 percent and median 3.0 percent. Our round numbers would thus be 5–6 percent for males and 2–3 percent for females."

Diamond, "Homosexuality and Bisexuality in Different Populations," 306.

- Laumann, et al., report: "Over 4 percent of the women [4.3 percent] and 9 percent of the men [9.1 percent] reported having engaged in at least one of these sexual practices ["oral sex" or "anything else sexual"] with a person of their own gender since puberty."

Laumann, et al., *The Social Organization of Sexuality*, 294–96.

Since age 18:

- The *Demography* study reported nearly identical results when sexual behavior is measured, finding that while 4.7 percent of men had at least one same-sex experience since age 18, "only 2.5 percent of men have engaged in exclusively same-sex sex over the year preceding the survey. Similarly, 3.5 percent of women have had at least one same-sex sexual experience, but only 1.4 percent have had exclusively same-sex sex over the year preceding the survey."

Black, et al., "Demographics of the Gay and Lesbian Population in the United States," 141.

Those claiming to have been exclusively involved in homosexual or lesbian behavior:

- Laumann, et al., found that "under 1 percent of all men (0.6 percent) have had sex only with other boys or men and never with a female partner. For women, the proportion is even smaller. About 5 percent of the women who have had female partners since puberty have never had sex with a male partner. This means that, overall, only 0.2 percent of all women had had sex only with women."

Laumann, et al., *The Social Organization of Sexuality*, 311–12.

- Billy, et al., report that a nationally representative study of the sexual behavior of men aged 20 to 39 in the United States shows that during the last ten years, "Approximately 1 percent [actually, 1.1 percent] of the men reported having had exclusively homosexual activity."

Billy, et al., "The Sexual Behavior of Men in the United States," 52, 59.

- The *Demography* study concludes: "Suppose we adopt the reasonably narrow definition of gay and lesbian to be individuals who have engaged in exclusively same-sex sex over the last year, [then] 2.5 percent of men are gay and 1.4 percent of women are lesbian."

Black, et al., "Demographics of the Gay and Lesbian Population in the United States," 147.

Those who engage in homosexual behavior (often for a temporary period of time) due to circumstances:

Finally, it is worth pointing out that some individuals, who are not homosexually-inclined, may be temporarily involved with homosexuality for various reasons, including curiosity or coercion:

- Men who engage in homosexuality only during their youth constitute a significant percentage of those who report homosexual behavior. Laumann, et al., found that those "who report same-gender sex only before they turn eighteen, not afterward, constitute 42 percent of the total number of men who report ever having a same-gender experience."

Laumann, et al., *The Social Organization of Sexuality*, 296.

- Gagnon and Simon also report that for over half of those men who had at least one homosexual experience, "this experience was before the age of fifteen and not after."

Gagnon and Simon, *Sexual Conduct*, pp. 131-32; cited in Laumann, et al., *The Social Organization of Sexuality*, 289, footnote 8.

- Fay et al., reporting in *Science* magazine, reached similar conclusions after analyzing data from a 1970 survey of American men age 21 or older. Forty-six percent of the men who reported "any homosexual experience" in their lifetimes reported that it occurred only prior to the age of 15 and not since. In addition, 24 percent of those reporting any lifetime homosexual experience reported they had had only one such experience. In fact, the number who reported they had had only one homosexual experience in their lifetime *and* that it had occurred before age 15 was *three times as high* as the number who had had homosexual experiences at age 20 or older and had them "fairly often."

Calculated from Tables 2 and 3 in Robert E. Fay, Charles F. Turner, Albert D. Klassen, John H. Gagnon, "Prevalence and Patterns of Same-Gender Sexual Contact among Men, *Science*, New Series, Vol. 243, Issue 4889 (20 January 1989): 341–42.

- Incarceration is another cause of "temporary" homosexual behavior. Noting that "many male respondents in the Kinsey surveys were prison inmates or had jail experiences," the *Archives of Sexual Behavior* study concludes: "Necessity might also force such behavior. In addition, any individual may exhibit heterosexual, homosexual, or bisexual behaviors for many reasons that have nothing to do with sexual arousal or interest. An individual, for example, may engage in homosexual or heterosexual activities for friendship, due to coercion or curiosity, or a host of other reasons…"

Diamond, "Homosexuality and Bisexuality in Different Populations," 298.

- Similarly, The *Social Organization of Sexuality* reports: "Some engage in sex with same-gender partners without any erotic or psychological desire because they have been forced or enticed into doing so. A classic example is sex in prison. [Being d]eprived of the opportunity to have sex with opposite-gender partners gives rise to same-gender sex, by volition or as the result of force."

Laumann, et al., *The Social Organization of Sexuality*, 291.

- *Sex in America* refers to the temporary nature of much homosexual activity: "Far more women and men experimented with homosexuality than currently identify themselves as lesbians or gays. It seems likely that many try it and then go back to being heterosexuals, neither desiring others of their own gender nor finding the idea of homosexual sex very appealing."

Michael, et al., *Sex in America*, 182.

The homosexual population as measured by those who exhibit all three aspects of same-gender sexuality: behavior, desire, and identity

- When all three possible aspects are taken together, we arrive at a low percentage of the population who are identified as homosexual. Laumann, et al., isolated "a core group (about 2.4 percent of the total men and about 1.3 percent of the total women) in our survey who define themselves as homosexual or bisexual, have same-gender partners, and express homosexual desires...."

Laumann, et al, *The Social Organization of Sexuality*, 300–301.

The Myth of "Exclusive" Homosexuality

Contrary to the common perception of homosexuals as those who are exclusively attracted to the same-sex, the research indicates that many homosexuals have also engaged in sexual relations with those of the opposite sex. This illustrates again the difficulty of precisely defining who should even be classified as "a homosexual." The evidence suggests that there is a substantial (though still quite small) population of people who experiment with homosexual behavior at some time in their lives. However, the percentage of people who are exclusively homosexual in their behavior throughout their lifetimes is extremely small indeed.

- The *Demography* study found that while "only a small fraction of heterosexual men and women ever have sex with a member of the same sex," homosexuals do not similarly shun heterosexual sex: "Gay men, however, typically have had sex with a woman, and lesbian women typically have had sex with a man, at some time since age 18." In particular, "among women who had at least one female sex partner since age 18, only 28 percent have been involved, over the past year, in exclusively same-sex sexual relationships. Similarly, only 42 percent of men who have had a male sexual partner since age 18 have had exclusively same-sex sex over the year before the survey."

Black, et al., "Demographics of the Gay and Lesbian Population in the United States," 141, 144.

- Laumann, et al., report that many homosexuals also have sexual experiences with and interest in people of the opposite gender as well. Their study found that in the past five years, about half of the men reporting same-sex sexual behavior "had both male and female partners in this time period. The women are more likely than the men to have had sex with both men and women [rather than with] only same-gender partners. Almost two-thirds of the women reporting a female partner in the past five years also report a male partner. The proportion of the men with male partners since age eighteen who report having had only male partners declines to about 20 percent of the total. For women, the comparable figure is about 10 percent."

Laumann, et al., *The Social Organization of Sexuality*, 311.

- As for lesbians, a survey of 6,935 women in the U.S. reported in the *Archives of Internal Medicine* found that "77.3 percent reported ever having had a male sexual partner, [and] 70.5 percent had engaged in vaginal intercourse at least once…"

Allison L. Diamant, Mark A. Schuster, Kimberly McGuigan, Janet Lever, "Lesbians' Sexual History with Men: Implications for Taking a Sexual History," *Archives of Internal Medicine* 159 (December 1999): 2,730–2,731.

- In fact, when the lifetime figures for *any* homosexual activity ("Any sex" in Chart 1 below) are compared with the lifetime figures for *exclusively* homosexual activity ("Since puberty" in Chart 2 below), we find that only about one in every 15 men with homosexual experience has been exclusively homosexual in behavior, while only about one in every 21 women with homosexual experience has been exclusively homosexual.

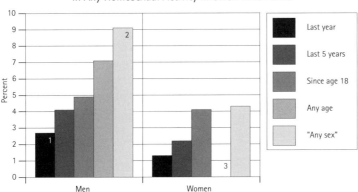

Chart 1: Percentage of People Who Have Engaged in *Any* Homosexual Activity in Given Time Period

1 The figures for these time periods are based on questions asking when they "had sex with a [person of the same sex]."

2 The figures for this category are based on a different question asking if the respondent had engaged in specific sex acts or "ever done anything else sexual" with a person of the same sex (Laumann et al., pp. 294, 674, 676).

3 Laumann et al. give a figure of 3.8 percent for this measure (p. 294 and Figure 8.1 on p. 295). However, this is logically inconsistent with the figure given in the previous category; it is impossible for the number who have had such sexual relations at "any age" to be *lower* than the number who have had such relations just "since age 18." Since Laumann et al. give no explanation for this discrepancy, we have omitted this lower figure from the chart.

Edward O. Laumann, John H. Gagnon, Robert T. Michael, and Stuart Michaels, *The Social Organization of Sexuality: Sexual Practices in the United States* (Chicago: The University of Chicago Press, 1994), 294–96.

Chart 2: Percentage of People Who Have Engaged in Exclusively Homosexual (and no Heterosexual) Activity in Given Time Period

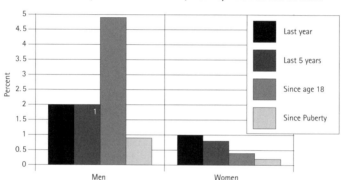

1 The fact that this figure is the same as the "last year" figure may seem anomalous, since one would expect exclusivity to decline with time. However, it may be explained by the fact that the percentages are of all respondents, including those who had *no* sexual activity in the given time period. Therefore, this figure may include men who have had *no* sexual relations in the *last* year, but have had exclusively homosexual relations during the last 5 years.

Edward O. Laumann, John H. Gagnon, Robert T. Michael, and Stuart Michaels, *The Social Organization of Sexuality: Sexual Practices in the United States* (Chicago: The University of Chicago Press, 1994), 310–312.

Homosexuality in Other Cultures

Researchers report similarly low percentages of homosexuals in other nations and cultures:

Europe:

- French and British surveys of sexual behavior reported in *Science* found that "homosexuality turns out to be significantly less common than suggested by Alfred Kinsey's survey." Alfred Spira, leader of the project that surveyed 20,000 French people between the ages of 18 and 69, found the percentage of homosexuals to be "rather low, in comparison to what I had expected." The *Science* report continues: "His group found that 4.1 percent of men and 2.6 percent of women said that they'd had homosexual intercourse at least once in their life. Only 1.1 percent of men and 0.3 percent of women said they'd had homosexual intercourse in the past 12 months. Those figures should help lay to rest myths about homosexuality that persist from Kinsey's survey..."

Peter Aldhous, "French Venture where U.S. Fears to Tread," *Science* 257 (July 3, 1992):25.

- Similarly, the *Archives of Sexual Behavior* reports: "Findings from a British national random study (Wellings *et al.*, 1990) also show low figures for homosexual activity....[O]nly 5 percent of men and 1 percent of women reported ever having a homosexual partner."

Diamond, "Homosexuality and Bisexuality in Different Populations," 302.

- The *Archives of Sexual Behavior* also found that a randomly selected population of Danish women personally interviewed by a female physician "found only 2 of 625 women [0.3 percent] from 22 to 70 years of age reporting having had a homosexual experience."

Ibid., 301.

- A survey of sexual behavior by the Dutch National Institute for Social Sexological Research and Utrecht University found, "In the preceding 12 months only 3.6 percent of the males and 0.3 percent of the females surveyed had exclusive same-sex contacts and an additional 1.9 percent of their male sample and 0.5 percent of their female sample had bisexual activities."

Ibid., 302.

Non-Western countries:

The *Archives of Sexual Behavior* study also examined homosexuality in other cultures and found similar percentages of homosexuals:

- One researcher in the Philippines found six male homosexuals and no lesbians in a village of 729 inhabitants. In addition, in the province of Siaton, with a population of 2,862, "there were 12 male homosexuals and 'several' lesbians." In another village with a with a population of approximately 18,000, "there were 70 openly homosexual males and 58 lesbians' (0.7 percent)."

- The report continues: "Recent research from Thailand by Sittitrai *et al.* (1992) reported similarly. Same-sex contact was reported by 3.3 percent of the males interviewed but only 0.2 percent indicated such behavior was exclusively homosexual. Among females 1.1 percent reported they had same-sex contact and 0.9 percent said it was exclusively so."

- A random sample of the population of the Republic of Palau found that "after the age of 20, homosexual activity was reported by 1.9 percent of the males and 2.8 percent of the females interviewed. Bisexual activity was reported by 2.8 percent of the males and 0.7 percent of the females." The study mentions, "In these nonhomophobic societies, Philippines, Thailand and Palau, it is interesting to note we find reported the lowest rates of same-sex activity."

- Diamond reports that in the first wide scale survey of China, "2.3 percent of 'peasants' and .5 percent of 'city dwellers' considered themselves gay."

Ibid., 301

What do Americans Believe About the Number of Homosexuals?

In spite of the overwhelming evidence above, the efforts to convince Americans that the homosexual population is large have been very effective.

- A survey of the American public conducted by Princeton Survey Research for the Kaiser Family Foundation found that only 14 percent of the general public correctly identified the size of the homosexual population as 3 percent or less. Seventy-two percent gave an exaggerated estimate, with at least 38 percent believing that homosexuals are actually *more* than 10 percent of the population. In fact, 8 percent guessed that over *40 percent* of Americans are homosexual. Ironically, however, the Kaiser survey itself showed that only

2 percent of those surveyed identified themselves as "gay or lesbian" and only 1 percent as "bisexual."

The Henry J. Kaiser Family Foundation, *Inside-OUT: A Report on the Experiences of Lesbians, Gays and Bisexuals in America and the Public's Views on Issues and Policies Related to Sexual Orientation* (November 2001), 5, 16; online at *http://www.kff.org/content/2001/3193/LGBToplines.pdf* (accessed October 22, 2003).

CHAPTER 3

Are Homosexuals a Disadvantaged Minority?

Homosexuals are certainly a minority group in American society—a tiny minority, in fact (see chapter 2 on "How Many Homosexuals Are There?"). And they may be said to suffer "discrimination," if the fact that a majority of the American people disapprove of same-sex sexual contact can be said to constitute "discrimination." However, most laws against "discrimination" target only discrimination that is irrational or intolerable because it is based on characteristics that are inborn, immutable, involuntary, innocuous, or in the Constitution. Race and sex are the classic examples; voluntary behavior patterns that are demonstrably harmful, such as homosexual acts, do not qualify for special protection.

Even with that distinction in mind, however, it is worth examining the claims of homosexual activists that they have experienced a long continuing history of pervasive discrimination and outright persecution. If any group in society has experienced such treatment, members of that group might be expected to be at a disadvantage with respect to various measures of achievement in society, such as education or income levels. Let's examine whether homosexuals suffer such disadvantages.

Education Levels among Homosexuals

Some minority groups in American society are at a clear disadvantage with respect to educational attainment. For example:

- According to the U. S. Census Bureau, as of 1998, 25.0 percent of white Americans had completed four years of college or more. However, only 14.7 percent of black Americans and 11.0 percent of Hispanics had the same level of educational attainment.

  U. S. Census Bureau, "Educational Attainment, by Race and Hispanic Origin: 1960 to 1998," *Statistical Abstract of the United States: 1999*, 119th edition (Washington, DC: October 1999), Table No. 263, 169.

However, studies indicate that homosexuals as a group actually have *higher* levels of education than heterosexuals.

- Michael, et al., report that homosexuals and lesbians tend to be more highly educated: "Our study shows that twice as many college-educated men identify themselves as homosexual as men with high-school educations, 3 percent of college-educated men said they were gay compared to 1.5 percent of men with high-school educations. For women the trend is even more striking. Women with college educations are eight times more likely to identify themselves as lesbians as are women with a high-school education. Four percent of female college graduates identify themselves as lesbians as compared to less than half a percent of female high-school graduates."

  Robert T. Michael, John H. Gagnon, Edward O. Laumann, and Gina Kolata, *Sex in America: A Definitive Survey* (Boston: Little, Brown and Co., 1994), 182.

- Laumann et al. add, "In general, women with high school degrees or less report very low rates of same-gender sexuality." On the other hand, women who have graduated from college always "report the highest level of same-gender sexuality." The authors conclude that "acceptance of nontraditional sexual behavior is likely to be higher among the more educated."

  Edward O. Laumann, John H. Gagnon, Robert T. Michael, and Stuart Michaels, *The Social Organization of Sexuality: Sexual Practices in the United States* (Chicago: The University of Chicago Press, 1994), 309.

- Similarly, a study in *Family Planning Perspectives* concludes that education was "positively associated with having had a same-gender sexual experience within the last ten years..."

  John O. G. Billy, Koray Tanfer, William R. Grady and Daniel H. Klepinger, "The Sexual Behavior of Men In the United States," *Family Planning Perspectives* 25, no. 2 (March/April 1993): 59.

- The Gay Financial Network reports that a readership survey of homosexual newspapers found higher levels of education and income among homosexuals as compared with the U.S. population as a whole: "The results of the paper's readership survey were highly impressive, with income and education levels significantly above that of the median population. Among its results, it found that 60 percent of readers were college graduates, compared to 18 percent for the general public."

Mike Wilke, "Commercial Closet: Are Gays All Rich?" 21 August, 2000, *http://www.gfn.com.*

- A study in *American Demographics* also found high education levels among homosexuals: "The precise size of the gay market may not be known, but the characteristics of gays make them prime consumer targets. The median educational attainment of gays is 15.7 years, compared with 12.7 for the overall adult U.S. population. Thirty-two percent of gays have attended college for four years or more, compared with 21 percent of the overall population."

J. Schwartz, "Gay Consumers Come Out Spending," *American Demographic*s 42 (April 1992): 10–11.

- A study on the income of homosexuals and lesbians in the *Journal of Policy Analysis and Management* reports: "[I]n our sample, men and women in same-sex couples have more education than people in different-sex couples."

Marieka M. Klawitter and Victor Flatt, "The Effects of State and Local Antidiscrimination Policies on Earnings for Gays and Lesbians," *Journal of Policy Analysis and Management*, 17 (4): 662 (1998).

- A study in *Sociological Perspectives* concludes that "gays overall, in fact, have higher educational attainment than comparable nongays. Their analysis of census data on couples finds that the average educational level for same-sex couples is above that of nongays." The study found that "65.7 percent of the respondents fall within the relatively narrow range of having a B.A. or an M.A., with only 7.9 percent reporting having no college, 19.1 percent reporting some college but no degree, and 7.2 percent having a Ph.D."

Donald C. Barrett, Lance M. Pollack, and Mary L. Tilden "Teenage Sexual Orientation, Adult Openness, and Status Attainment in Gay Males," *Sociological Perspectives*, 45 (2002): 166, 170.

Income Levels among Homosexuals

If a minority group has experienced a long history of pervasive discrimination and persecution (as homosexuals claim to have done), members of that group might be expected to have lower average incomes than the rest of the population. For example, 1999 Census Bureau statistics showed that 23.6 percent of black Americans live in poverty, compared to only 9.8 percent of white Americans.

> Bureau of the Census, U. S. Department of Commerce, "Poverty by Family Status, Sex, and Race, 1986–99," in *The World Almanac and Book of Facts 2002* (New York: World Almanac Education Group, Inc., 2002), 388.

However, a similar comparison of the incomes of homosexuals and heterosexuals does not produce a similar result:

- "A measure often used to demonstrate sex or race discrimination—individual or household income—reveals an unexpected pattern. Surveys that collect such data usually find incomes for the lesbian and/or gay respondents that are higher than the national averages."

> M.V. Lee Badgett and Rhonda M. Williams, "The Economics of Sexual Orientation: Establishing a Research Agenda," *Feminist Studies* 18 (3): 649–657 (Fall 1992).

A Study in Contradictions

Actually, homosexual advocates alternately portray two competing, mutually contradictory images of the homosexual community. One is that of homosexuals as an affluent "niche" market that demands special consideration by Madison Avenue and corporations. The other is the portrayal of homosexuals as suffering economic discrimination—an argument offered in support of their demands for special legal protections.

- A study in *Gay & Lesbian Review Worldwide* downplays the former "image": "It has been widely reported over the last decade that gay and lesbian consumers constitute a more affluent market on average than non-gay American households. Meanwhile, in reaction to these (often exaggerated) claims concerning gay affluence, the opposite argument is now being advanced, namely that gay and lesbian consumers are actually less affluent than their non-gay counterparts."

> Howard Buford, "Understanding Gay Consumers," *Gay & Lesbian Review Worldwide*, 7 (Spring 2000): 26–28.

- Similarly, a report in the *Contra Costa Times* comments on the two competing images: "Who's right? A dearth of reliable demographic data on the gay market makes it hard to tell. But the debate is increasingly contentious and has created rifts within the gay community. Marketers say gay Americans should be recognized as a vibrant segment of the consumer market. But civil-rights advocates maintain that an exaggerated image of comfort and success hurts their battles for protection from workplace discrimination, the right to marry and other causes."

Ronald Alsop, "Gay's Affluence Data Contradicted; Are Homosexuals More Affluent than Others? Some Activists Suggest that the Data are Overstated," *Contra Costa Times* (January 16, 2000): D1.

- The *Gay and Lesbian Review Worldwide* study mentions those who attempt to "benefit by claiming that the gay market was extravagantly more affluent and better educated than mainstream America....More recently still, the opposite claims are being made by people who prefer to present lesbians and gay men as a "marginalized" or oppressed minority."

Buford, "Understanding Gay Consumers," 26–28.

- *Business Week* makes much the same point: "A common perception, especially among marketing experts, is that gays are far more affluent than other groups. Not so, say many who favor laws banning workplace discrimination based on sexual orientation. Gays, they claim, are often discriminated against by employers."

Gene Koretz, "Do Gays Have Higher Incomes?" *Business Week* 21 (April 2003): 30.

Do homosexuals earn less—or more?

Conclusive evidence to answer this question once and for all may simply not be available. As one observer wrote:

- "The fact is, we don't know with certainty how gay and lesbian affluence compares to that of the general public, because studies to date have not satisfied the rigors of sound methodology."

Howard Buford, "Understanding Gay Consumers," *Gay & Lesbian Review Worldwide*, 7 (2): 26–28 (Spring 2000).

However, this uncertainty has not prevented one pro-homosexual researcher from dedicating much of her professional career to decrying what she calls the "myth" of homosexual affluence. M.V. Lee Badgett, professor of economics at the University of Massachusetts, argues that:

- "[L]esbians and gay men earn no more than heterosexual people; indeed, in some cases gay men appear to earn less than comparable heterosexual men."

M. V. Lee Badgett, *Income Inflation: The Myth of Affluence Among Gay, Lesbian, and Bisexual Americans*, (National Gay and Lesbian Task Force and the Institute for Gay and Lesbian Strategic Studies: 1998): 2.

Badgett is also the Director of the Institute for Gay and Lesbian Strategic Studies, a "think tank" associated with the National Gay and Lesbian Task Force, a pro-homosexual political activist organization. This strong bias should always be considered when weighing her research.

Ways of Measuring Affluence

No one measure of income is sufficient for analyzing this issue. Because women's earnings are different from men's, we can likewise differences in income between male homosexuals and lesbians. In addition, measuring the income of individual earners yields a different result from measures of total household income (i.e., the combined income of workers who live together).

As measured by individual income, there are indications that homosexual men may earn less than heterosexual men.

While the data appear to be inconclusive, some research does indicate that homosexual men earn slightly less than do heterosexual men. Pro-homosexual activist M. V. Lee Badgett, however, is the source of most of these claims.

- For example, in one study she claims that the "average gay man earns from 4 percent to 7 percent less than the average heterosexual man."

Badgett, "The Myth of Gay & Lesbian Affluence," 22–25.

- In another article, she reports: "By analyzing pooled 1989–1991 data from a national random sample, the General Social Survey, it is found that gay and bisexual male workers earned from 11 percent to 27 percent less than heterosexual male workers with the same experience, education, occupation, marital status, and region of residence."

M. V. Lee Badgett, "The Wage Effects of Sexual Orientation Discrimination," *Industrial & Labor Relations Review*, 48 (4): 726 (July 1995).

- *Business Week* reported one of the few studies by someone other than Badgett with similar findings: "Based on six years of survey data from the 1990s, a recent study by economists Nathan Berg of the University of Texas at Dallas and Donald Lien of the University of Texas at San Antonio finds that gay men earn about 22 percent less than similarly qualified straight men, controlling for such variables as age, race, education, occupation, and area of residence."

Gene Koretz, "Do Gays Have Higher Incomes?" *Business Week*, 21 April 2003, 30.

Is discrimination the reason homosexual men may earn less?

Even if it is true that the individual income of homosexual men is less, there are a number of factors other than discrimination that could be the cause. For example:

- **Workforce participation.** A study in the *Journal of Policy Analysis and Management* offers the following explanation as to why homosexual men often earn less: "Gay men, unlike heterosexual men, may share their home with other males and pool two male-sized incomes. Because of this income-sharing, and perhaps in anticipation of not serving as a primary household earner, gay men might devote less time and effort to the labor market."

Klawitter and Flatt, "The Effects of State and Local Antidiscrimination Policies on Earnings for Gays and Lesbians," 662.

- **Occupational choice.** Barrett et al., in *Sociological Perspectives*, reported that "occupation selection had the greatest negative effect on the incomes of men who could be defined as gay. In particular, men who could be defined as gay and in traditionally female-dominated jobs earned the least." They concluded that ""[G]ay males may be likely to self-select career paths in traditionally lower status and lower income female-dominated occupations."

Donald C. Barrett, Lance M. Pollack, and Mary L. Tilden "Teenage Sexual Orientation, Adult Openness, and Status Attainment in Gay Males," *Sociological Perspectives*, 45 (2): 168 (2002).

- **Marital status.** Barrett et al. report a 1990 study that found that "both gay men and unmarried heterosexuals...had lower income than married heterosexuals." They also note a 2001 study that "the majority of the difference between gay men and nongays can be considered to derive from" their marital status, "rather than their sexual orientation." Barrett et al. agree with this conclusion, noting "it may be that any negative or positive effects due to openness [about a homosexual orientation] are relatively limited and that the actual causes for reduced income of gay men may result from their status as single, not their status as gay."

  Barrett, *et al.*, "Teenage Sexual Orientation, Adult Openness, and Status Attainment in Gay Males," 165, 166, 178–79.

Other research, however, indicates that "households" headed by homosexual men actually have higher incomes

- In the case of one study, high incomes were noted even in "households" consisting of only one homosexual man. *Sociological Perspectives* reports: "The average household income in the sample is also high and remains high even if analysis is limited to those who do not have a live-in partner (51.6 percent of those without a partner reported a household income of $40,000 or more.)"

  Barrett, *et al.*, "Teenage Sexual Orientation, Adult Openness, and Status Attainment in Gay Males," 175.

- Even Badgett has admitted the increased earning power of homosexual male couples. "The Census results show that male same-sex couples have household incomes 24 percent higher than married couples," she reports.

  M.V. Lee Badgett, *Income Inflation: The Myth of Affluence Among Gay, Lesbian, and Bisexual Americans*, (New York: The Policy Institute of the National Gay and Lesbian Task Force and The Institute for Gay and Lesbian Strategic Studies, 1998), 15.

- A study in the *Journal of Policy Analysis and Management* reports: "Regardless of the level of employment protection, male same-sex couples had the highest household incomes, followed by married couples, female same-sex couples, and unmarried different-sex couples."

  Klawitter and Flatt, "The Effects of State and Local Antidiscrimination Policies on Earnings for Gays and Lesbians," 669.

Lesbian incomes

As the quote above indicates, there is some evidence that female same-sex couples have lower household incomes than married couples. However, once again, the reason probably has less to do with discrimination based on sexual orientation than with a more basic factor—being female. Even Badgett concedes this:

- "In 1996, the typical woman working full-time, all year round, still earned only 74 percent of a man's income. So we would expect the average household income of a female couple to be less than the income of a typical male-female couple…"

  M.V. Lee Badgett, *Income Inflation: The Myth of Affluence Among Gay, Lesbian, and Bisexual Americans,* (New York: The Policy Institute of the National Gay and Lesbian Task Force and The Institute for Gay and Lesbian Strategic Studies, 1998), 15.

- It is also notable that despite this factor, Klawitter and Flatt found that "female same-sex couples" still earned more than "unmarried different-sex couples."

  Klawitter and Flatt, "The Effects of State and Local Antidiscrimination Policies on Earnings for Gays and Lesbians," 669.

As measured by individual income, lesbians earn more than heterosexual women

- Even Badgett, a chief proponent of the "income disparity based on discrimination" theory, is forced to admit that when it comes to lesbians, according to the 1990 U.S. Census "the average woman with a female partner earns more than the average heterosexual woman does."

  Badgett, "The Myth of Gay & Lesbian Affluence," 22–25.

- *Sociological Perspectives* agrees: "Limited research on lesbians," they note, "suggests that they may make more than comparable heterosexual women."

  Barrett, *et al.,* "Teenage Sexual Orientation, Adult Openness, and Status Attainment in Gay Males," 164.

- The *Journal of Policy Analysis and Management* also reports that even in areas without laws to forbid employment discrimination based on sexual orientation, "women in same-sex couples earned about 18 percent more" than married women.

Marieka M. Klawitter and Victor Flatt, "The Effects of State and Local Antidiscrimination Policies on Earnings for Gays and Lesbians," *Journal of Policy Analysis and Management*, 17 (4): 674 (1998).

- The same University of Texas study that found homosexual men earning less than heterosexuals also found that "gay women earn approximately 30 percent more than similarly qualified heterosexual women."

Gene Koretz, "Do Gays Have Higher Incomes?" *Business Week*, 21 April 2003, 30.

Household Income According to Marketing Surveys

The evidence may be mixed regarding the individual income of homosexuals compared with heterosexuals. However, a number of marketing surveys have given indication that combined household income of gays and lesbians is higher than that of married households.

Some critics claim that not too much weight should be placed on market surveys, because they often use data drawn from an unrepresentative sample of the homosexual population, such as particular mailing lists.

- Badgett argues, for example, that "gay men and lesbians surveyed from samples of magazine readers have higher-than-average incomes compared to all Americans, but this does not translate into higher average incomes for gay and lesbian people in general."

M.V. Lee Badgett, "The Myth of Gay & Lesbian Affluence," *Gay & Lesbian Review Worldwide*, 7 (2): 22–25 (Spring 2000).

However, even viewed with such caution, many of the marketing studies have shown impressive results, and make clear that many homosexuals are doing very well economically.

- An Internet survey of nearly 6,000 homosexuals and lesbians conducted jointly by the gay and lesbian market research firm Opus-Comm Group, Syracuse University, and the media/entertainment company GSociety, Inc., reports: "The median combined household income of gay couples is $65,000, nearly 60 percent higher than the 1999 U.S. median income of $40,800....More than a fifth of respondents reported a total combined income of $100,000 or more. Nearly 60 percent of gay male households and 46 percent of lesbian households showed a combined income in excess of $60,000."

"Gay Purchasing Power a Significant Force, Major Study Reveals," News Release:OpusComm Group, Inc. (October 17, 2001).

The higher household incomes of homosexuals and lesbians is confirmed by the "gay-friendly" marketing firm Rainbow Referrals:

- "21 percent of Gay and Lesbian households have income greater than $100,000 per year. This represents a greater household income versus the average U.S. household income."

- "28 percent of Gay and Lesbian households have income greater than $50,000 per year. This represents a greater household income versus the average U.S. household income."

Furthermore, homosexuals are:

- "Twice as likely to have household income over $60,000 than general U.S. population."

- "Twice as likely to have household income over $250,000 than general U.S. population."

This leads to the conclusion that the "gay market:"

- "Consists of the most economically advantaged people in the U.S."

"National Marketing Studies Confirm the Affluence of the Gay and Lesbian Market," 23 April 2003, *http://www.rainbowreferrals.com.*

Their incomes and spending patterns make homosexuals a coveted market

- The *Philadelphia Inquirer* reports: "Community Marketing reports that gays and lesbians spend $54 billion a year on travel, and that 91 percent take yearly vacations, compared with the national average of 64 percent. And, when traveling, they spend at least $1,500 per person."

Linda K. Harris, "Philadelphia Finds a New Travel Clique," *The Philadelphia Inquirer*, 20 April 2003.

The marketing firm Rainbow Referrals cites data gleaned from national marketing studies that confirms the affluence of the gay and lesbian market, described as a "relatively untapped, lucrative and extremely brand loyal market." These "gay-market facts" concerning the spending habits of homosexuals and lesbians include:

- Over 90 percent of homosexuals and lesbians took a domestic trip during the year of research study.

- 60 percent took a foreign trip in the last 3 years.

- They are three times more likely to be online than the average American (1997).

- They are four times as likely to spend over $150 on long distance monthly.

- They are twice as likely to spend $250 on cellular service.

- 65 percent identify themselves as having to have the "latest."

- 68 percent readily upgrade to a product's latest model.

- 77 percent "believe in indulging themselves."

- 57 percent "prefer to buy top-of-the-line."

- 59 percent describe themselves as buying for themselves whatever they want.

"National Marketing Studies Confirm the Affluence of the Gay and Lesbian Market," 23 April 2003, *http://www.rainbowreferrals.com.*

Homosexuals and lesbians enjoy higher disposable income because they are unfettered by the expenses of rearing children

The homosexual community enjoys higher discretionary income largely because it has absolved itself of participating in one of society's most vitally important functions: the rearing of the next generation.

- The *Gay Financial Network* reports: "Gay people are said to have higher disposable incomes chiefly because they don't appear as likely to raise children. They gay community was charmingly known for a while in the marketing industry as DINKS, short for Double Income, No Kids."

Mike Wilke, "Commercial Closet: Are Gays All Rich?" 21 August, 2000, *http://www.gfn.com*.

- According to *Journal of Policy Analysis and Management,* lesbians are also comparatively unfettered by the rearing of children, which provides them with an advantage in the workplace: "Lesbians…may choose to get more education and to devote more time and energy to the labor market than heterosexual women. Lesbian couples are also much less likely than married women to be living with children. (Child-rearing responsibilities cut into time and energy to devote to market work.)"

Klawitter and Flatt, "The Effects of State and Local Antidiscrimination Policies on Earnings for Gays and Lesbians," 662.

- Sarah Craig of Overlooked Opinions, a marketing firm that surveys gay consumers, reports in *American Demographics*: "Businesses have overlooked the fact that gay people often have more discretionary income….They also travel more often simply because they have no children. 'Gays can take a job transfer without thinking about schools or child care,' she says."

Schwartz, "Gay Consumers Come Out Spending," 10–11.

- Syracuse University professor Amy Falkner, cited in the Opus-Comm study, concurs: "This means well-heeled gay and lesbian couples, sharing two incomes and generally without the expense of raising children (13 percent of Gay/Lesbian couples have children under 18 years of age living at home), can plan to be actively courted in the near future by industry and services anxious to open up this "new" market," says Falkner.

Falkner, "Gay Purchasing Power a Significant Force," 2.

- The *Gay and Lesbian Review Worldwide* elaborates: "Two lifestyle facts in particular account for much of the difference in the gay community's patterns of consumption: higher discretionary income and more disposable time. The absence of children in the vast majority of gay households means that these households, which probably do not earn dramatically more than others in the U.S., do have dramatically more discretionary income, that is, money that's not earmarked for necessities like feeding and clothing the kids and paying for their health care. An even stronger effect of the absence of children is a gain in disposable time. Today's "supermom"—or dad—devote much of their non-working time to child care, while gay and lesbian consumers are more likely to have time for leisure activities, and are thus especially interesting prospects for products and services that are consumed in units of disposable time. This includes entertainment and travel and all the industries they encompass, such as movies, premium TV channels, airlines, cruise companies, resorts, and so on."

Buford, "Understanding Gay Consumers," 26–28.

Prohibiting discrimination against homosexuals would have little effect in improving their income relative to heterosexuals

Pro-homosexual activists claim that homosexuals are disadvantaged relative to heterosexuals (even though the evidence with respect to income is mixed on that score, as we have seen). They also contend that laws barring "discrimination" based on "sexual orientation" are necessary and valuable in order to improve the economic status of the homosexual population.

There is evidence that such legal protections have boosted the economic position of some other groups in society:

- "Researchers have judged the federal-level antidiscrimination policies in the Civil Rights Act of 1964 and subsequent revisions to have moderate but measurable effects on earnings for women and ethnic minorities."

  Marieka M. Klawitter and Victor Flatt, "The Effects of State and Local Antidiscrimination Policies on Earnings for Gays and Lesbians," *Journal of Policy Analysis and Management*, 17 (4): 659 (1998).

However, contrary to what might be expected, Klawitter and Flatt found that neither private nondiscrimination policies nor public anti-discrimination laws based on sexual orientation have the same effect:

- "In contrast to studies of antidiscrimination laws for women and ethnic minorities, we have produced no evidence that employment protections for sexual orientation directly increase average earnings for members of same-sex households."

  Marieka M. Klawitter and Victor Flatt, "The Effects of State and Local Antidiscrimination Policies on Earnings for Gays and Lesbians," *Journal of Policy Analysis and Management*, 17 (4): 676 (1998).

CHAPTER 4

Is Homosexuality a Health Risk?

Portraying homosexuality as harmless is a key goal of homosexual activists, as homosexual author Urvashi Vaid has admitted:

- "We have an agenda to create a society in which homosexuality is regarded as healthy, natural, and normal. To me that is the most important agenda item."

  Quoted in Gabriel Rotello, *Sexual Ecology: AIDS and the Destiny of Gay Men* (New York: Penguin Books, 1997), 286.

The reality, however, is quite the opposite, as was recently conceded by the homosexual newspaper *New York Blade News*:

- "Reports at a national conference about sexually transmitted diseases indicate that gay men are in the highest risk group for several of the most serious diseases....Scientists believe that the increased number of sexually transmitted diseases (STD) cases is the result of an increase in risky sexual practices by a growing number of gay men who believe HIV is no longer a life-threatening illness."

  Bill Roundy, "STD Rates on the Rise," *New York Blade News, (*December 15, 2000), 1.

This chapter will examine the significantly elevated health problems experienced by homosexuals, most of them the direct consequence of engaging in specific sexual acts and behavior patterns (such as having multiple sexual partners) that are common among homosexuals.

One warning—because of the subject matter, parts of this chapter are quite graphic in their description of specific sexual acts and their health consequences. Some readers may find this disturbing.

HIV/AIDS in the Homosexual Community

The human immunodeficiency virus (HIV) is responsible for causing AIDS, for which there exists no cure.

Homosexuals at increased risk for contracting HIV

- "In a large CDC study, conducted in sexually transmitted disease (STD) clinics in five major U.S. cities, researchers found the rate of new HIV infections among men who have sex with men (MSM) to be nine times higher than among women and heterosexual men. According to other CDC research, a number of factors contribute to high rates of infection among MSM, including psychosocial problems like depression and illicit drug use, age of sexual partners, and low rates of HIV testing among young MSM, particularly African Americans."

  "New CDC Studies Shed Light on Factors Underlying High HIV Infection Rates Among Gay and Bisexual Men," CDC Press Release (July 9, 2002).

Homosexual men are the largest risk category

- The CDC reports that homosexuals comprise the single largest exposure category of the more than 660,000 males with AIDS in the United States. As of December 2001, "men who have sex with men" and "men who have sex with men and inject drugs" together accounted for 63 percent of the cumulative total of male AIDS cases.

  "Table 9. Male Adult/Adolescent AIDS Cases by Exposure Category and Race/Ethnicity, Reported through December 2001, United States," Centers for Disease Control and Prevention: Division of HIV/AIDS Prevention: available at: *www.cdc.gov/hiv/stats/hasr1302.pdf.*

Homosexuals with HIV are at increased risk for developing other life-threatening diseases

- A paper delivered at the Fourth International AIDS Malignancy Conference at the National Institutes of Health reported that homosexual men with HIV have "a 37-fold increase in anal cancer, a 4-fold increase in Hodgkin's disease (cancer of the lymph nodes), a

2.7-fold increase in cancer of the testicles, and a 2.5-fold increase in lip cancer."

"Studies Point to Increased Risks of Anal Cancer," *The Washington Blade* (June 2, 2000). Available at: *www.washblade.com/health/000602hm.*

HIV/AIDS and young people

- AIDS incidence is on the rise among teens and young adults. The CDC reports that, "even though AIDS incidence (the number of new cases diagnosed during a given time period, usually a year) is declining, *there has not been a comparable decline in the number of newly diagnosed HIV cases among youth.*

  "Young People at Risk: HIV/AIDS among America's Youth," Divisions of HIV/AIDS Prevention Centers for Disease Control (November 14, 2000).

- Young homosexual men are at particular risk. The CDC estimates that "at least half of all new HIV infections in the United States are among people under twenty-five, and the majority of [those infected] are infected sexually."

  Ibid.

- By the end of 1999, 29,629 young people aged thirteen to twenty-four were diagnosed with AIDS in the United States. MSM were the single largest risk category. In 1999, for example, 50 percent of all new AIDS cases were reported among young homosexuals.

  Ibid.

Dangerous sexual behavior among homosexuals

The high rates of HIV infection among homosexual men are largely due to two behavioral factors—the practice of anal intercourse, which facilitates the transfer of the virus far more easily than vaginal intercourse, and the practice of having sexual relations with multiple sex partners, which multiplies the opportunities for both acquiring and transmitting HIV.

- It is generally agreed that the sexual partner who plays the receptive role in an act of insertive sexual intercourse is at the greater risk of infection with HIV. The fact that anal intercourse poses a far greater risk than vaginal intercourse was documented in an article in the prestigious *New England Journal of Medicine*, co-authored by none other than Julie Louise Gerberding—now Director of the Centers for Disease Control. The article said, "The probability of HIV transmission associated with unprotected receptive anal intercourse" ranges from "0.008 to 0.032," or between 1 in 125 and 1 in 31 (for each such act). Meanwhile, the probability of HIV transmission for unprotected vaginal intercourse ranges from "0.0005 to 0.0015," or between 1 in 2000 and 1 in 666. This suggests that anal intercourse is *at least* five times more dangerous, and possibly as much as 64 times more dangerous, with a mid-range estimate of 16 to 21 times more dangerous than vaginal intercourse.

Mitchell H. Katz, M.D. and Julie Louise Gerberding, M.D., "Postexposure Treatment of People Exposed to the Human Immunodeficiency Virus through Sexual Contact or Injection-Drug Use," *The New England Journal of Medicine* 336, no. 15 (April 10, 1997), 1097.

Despite two decades of intensive efforts to educate homosexuals against the dangers of acquired immunodeficiency syndrome (AIDS) and other STDs, the incidence of unsafe sexual practices that often result in various diseases is on the rise.

- "The proportion of surveyed MSM (Men who have sex with men) who reported having had anal sex increased from 57.6 percent…in 1994 to 61.2 percent in 1997…the proportion reporting 'always' using condoms declined from 69:6 percent in 1994 to 60.8 per-cent…in 1997."

  "Increases in Unsafe Sex and Rectal Gonorrhea among Men Who Have Sex with Men—San Francisco, California, 1994–1997," *Mortality and Morbidity Weekly Report*, Centers for Disease Control and Prevention, (January 29, 1999), 45.

- "The proportion of men reporting having multiple sex partners and UAI (unprotected anal sex) increased from 23.6 percent…in 1994 to 33.3 percent…in 1997….The largest increase in this category (from 22 percent to 33.3 percent) was reported by respondents aged less than or equal to 25 years…"

  "Increases in Unsafe Sex and Rectal Gonorrhea among Men Who Have Sex with Men—San Francisco, California, 1994–1997," 45.

- "There has been a resurgence of gonorrhea (GC) and syphilis among men who have sex with men (MSM), as well as decreasing use of condoms during receptive anal intercourse (RAI)….These data identify a relatively high prevalence of STDs among the MSM pre-senting for medical care and STD screening. Of particular concern is the HIV prevalence among those with STDs, indicating recent unsafe sexual activities among these men."

"Abstract 321 from the 2002 National STD Prevention Conference 'Sexually Transmitted Diseases, HIV Testing, and HIV Risk Behaviors Among Men Who Have Sex with Men Seeking Care at Howard Brown Health Center'," National Center for HIV, STD and TB Prevention Division of Sexually Transmitted Diseases (March 5, 2002).

- A study of 4,300 gay or bisexual men in six U.S. cities published in the *American Journal of Public Health* found: "Among 4,295 men, 48.0 percent and 54.9 percent, respectively, reported unprotected receptive and insertive anal sex in the previous 6 months. Unprotected sex was significantly more likely with 1 primary partner or multiple partners than with 1 nonprimary partner. Drug and alcohol use were significantly associated with unprotected anal sex."

Beryl A. Koblin, et al, "High-Risk Behaviors among Men Who Have Sex With Men in 6 US Cities: Baseline Data From the EXPLORE Study," *American Journal of Public Health* 93 (June, 2003): 926–932.

Younger homosexuals at risk

Following in the footsteps of the generation of homosexuals decimated by AIDS, younger homosexuals are engaging in dangerous sexual practices at an alarming rate.

- The *Journal of the American Medical Association (JAMA)* surveyed 3,492 15- to 22-year-old MSM, reporting: "It is sobering that 41 percent of all the men had had unprotected anal sex during the past 6 months. It is also sobering that 37 percent of the HIV-infected men who did not know they were infected…and 13 percent of the HIV-infected men who did know they were HIV infected…reported unprotected insertive anal sex during the past 6 months."

Linda A. Valleroy, et al., "HIV Prevalence and Associated Risks in Young Men Who Have Sex with Men," *JAMA* 284 (July 12, 2000): 203.

- The John Hopkins University School of Public Health interviewed 361 gay and bisexual men age 15 to 22 and found that "37 percent said they had not used a condom for anal sex during their last sexual encounter with another male. Twenty-one percent reported having been high on drugs or alcohol during their last same-sex encounter."

Jon Garbo, "Risky Sex Common among Gay Club and Bar Goers," *GayHealth News* (January 3, 2001).

- A Johns Hopkins University School of Public Health study of three-hundred-sixty-one young men who have sex with men (MSM) aged fifteen to twenty-two found that around 40 percent of participants reported having had anal-insertive sex, and around 30 percent said they had had anal-receptive sex. Thirty-seven percent said they had not used a condom for anal sex during their last same-sex encounter. Twenty-one percent of the respondents reported using drugs or alcohol during their last same-sex encounter.

Garbo, Ibid.

- A five-year CDC study of 3,492 homosexual males aged fifteen to twenty-two found that "a quarter of those men, aged 15 to 22, said they recently had unprotected sex with both men and women." Another CDC study of 1,942 homosexual and bisexual men with HIV found that "at least 19 percent had at least one episode of unprotected anal sex—the riskiest sexual behavior—in the year before in 1998 and 1997. That is a 50 percent rise from 1995 and 1996..."

"Bisexuals Serve as 'Bridge' Infecting Women With HIV," *Reuters News Service* (July 30, 2000).

Homosexuals failing to disclose their HIV status to sex partners

- A study presented July 13, 2000, at the XIII International AIDS Conference in Durban, South Africa, disclosed that significant numbers of homosexual and bisexual men with HIV "continue to engage in unprotected sex with people who have no idea they could be contracting HIV....16 percent of gay men who were included in a nationwide sample of 1,397 HIV-positive people receiving medical care reported having at least one episode of unprotected sex with an unaware partner in the last six months."

Ulysses Torassa, "Some With HIV Aren't Disclosing Before Sex; UCSF Researcher's 1,397-person Study Presented During AIDS Conference," *The San Francisco Examiner* (July 15, 2000).

- Researchers from the University of California, San Francisco, found that "36 percent of homosexuals who engaged in unprotected oral, anal, or vaginal sex did not disclose their serostatus to casual sex partners."

Garbo, "Gay and Bi Men Less Likely to Disclose They Have HIV."

- Similarly, a study of HIV positive bisexual men in Los Angeles "found that 54.5 percent failed to disclose their infection status to sex partners. Thirty-one percent reported having unprotected sex."

- A CDC report revealed that, in 1997, 45 percent of homosexuals reporting having had unprotected anal intercourse during the previous six months did not know the HIV serostatus of all their sex partners. Even more alarming, among those who reported having had unprotected anal intercourse *and multiple partners*, 68 percent did not know the HIV serostatus of their partners.

Garbo, Ibid.

Unhealthy aspects of "monogamous" homosexual relationships

Even those homosexual relationships that are loosely termed "monogamous" do not necessarily result in healthier behavior.

- The exclusivity of the relationship did not diminish the incidence of unhealthy sexual acts, which are commonplace among homosexuals. An English study published in the same issue of the journal *AIDS* concurred, finding that most "unsafe" sex acts among homosexuals occur in steady relationships.

G. J. Hart et al., "Risk Behaviour, Anti-HIV and Anti-Hepatitis B Core Prevalence in Clinic and Non-clinic Samples of Gay Men in England, 1991–1992," *AIDS*, July 1993, 863–869, cited in "Homosexual Marriage: The Next Demand," Position Analysis paper by Colorado for Family Values (May 1994).

Homosexuals and Other Sexually-Transmitted Diseases (STDs)

- STDs are rampant in the homosexual community. The Centers for Disease Control reports: "Several recent reports have documented alarming increases in sexually transmitted infection rates among men who have sex with men (MSM), and a corresponding decline in safer sex practices. After years of successful prevention efforts, this trend may portend a resurgence of HIV infection in the MSM community."

"Abstract 418 from the 2002 National STD Prevention Conference 'Patterns of STD Infection, HIV Coinfection, and Risk-Behavior among MSM at a Boston Community Health Center'," National Center for HIV, STD and TB Prevention Division of Sexually Transmitted Diseases (March 5, 2002).

Human Papillomavirus (HPV)

HPV is a collection of more than seventy types of viruses that can cause warts, or papillomas, on various parts of the body. More than twenty types of HPV are incurable STDs that can infect the genital tract of both men and women. Most HPV infections are subclinical or asymptomatic, with only one in a hundred people experiencing genital warts.

- **HPV is "almost universal" among homosexuals.** According to the homosexual newspaper The *Washington Blade*: "A San Francisco study of Gay and bisexual men revealed that HPV infection was almost universal among HIV-positive men, and that 60 percent of HIV-negative men carried HPV."

  Bill Roundy, "STDs Up Among Gay Men: CDC Says Rise is Due to HIV Misperceptions."

- **HPV can lead to anal cancer.** At the recent Fourth International AIDS Malignancy Conference at the National Institutes of Health, Dr. Andrew Grulich announced that "most instances of anal cancer are caused by a cancer-causing strain of HPV through receptive anal intercourse. HPV infects over 90 percent of HIV-positive gay men and 65 percent of HIV-negative gay men, according to a number of recent studies."

  Richard A. Zmuda, "Rising Rates of Anal Cancer for Gay Men," *Cancer News* (August 17, 2000). Available at: *cancerlinksusa.com/cancernews_sm/Aug2000 / 081700analcancer.*

- **The link between HPV and cervical cancer.** Citing a presentation by Dr. Stephen Goldstone to the International Congress on Papillomavirus in Human Pathology in Paris, the *Washington Blade* reports that "HPV is believed to cause cervical cancer in women."

  "Studies Point to Increased Risks of Anal Cancer," *The Washington Blade* (June 2, 2000). Available at: *www.washblade.com/health/000602hm.*

Hepatitis

This is a potentially fatal liver disease that increases the risk of liver cancer.

- **Hepatitis A:** The *Mortality and Morbidity Weekly Report* published by the CDC reports: "Outbreaks of hepatitis A among men who have sex with men are a recurring problem in many large cities in the industrialized world."

Mortality and Morbidity Weekly Report, Centers for Disease Control and Prevention (September 4, 1998), 708.

- "Men who have sex with men (MSM) are at an increased risk of becoming infected with hepatitis A virus (HAV). Outbreaks of hepatitis A continue among MSM in large urban areas and surveillance data suggest that at least 10 percent of acute HAV infections are among MSM."

"Health Professionals Should not Miss an Opportunity to Vaccinate Men Who Have Sex with Men against hepatitis A and hepatitis B," Centers for Disease Control National Center for Infectious Diseases (March 3, 2003).

- **Hepatitis B:** This is a serious disease caused by a virus that attacks the liver. The virus, which is called hepatitis B virus (HBV), can cause lifelong infection, cirrhosis (scarring) of the liver, liver cancer, liver failure, and death. Each year in the United States, more than 200,000 people of all ages contract hepatitis B and close to 5,000 die of sickness caused by AIDS. The CDC reports that MSM are at increased risk for hepatitis B.

"Viral Hepatitus B—Frequently Asked Questions," National Center for Infectious Diseases, Centers for Disease Control and Prevention (September 29, 2000).

- "Men who have sex with men are also at risk for acquiring hepatitis B. Approximately 15 percent of all new hepatitis B virus (HBV) infections are among MSM."

"Health Professionals Should not Miss an Opportunity to Vaccinate Men Who Have Sex with Men against hepatitis A and hepatitis B," Centers for Disease Control National Center for Infectious Diseases (March 3, 2003).

- **Hepatitis C** is an inflammation of the liver that can cause cirrhosis, liver failure and liver cancer. The virus can lie dormant in the body for up to thirty years before flaring up. Although less so than with hepatitis A and B, MSM who engage in unsafe sexual practices remain at increased risk for contracting hepatitis C.

"Hepatitus C: Epidemiology: Transmission Modes," *Mortality and Morbidity Weekly Report,* Centers for Disease Control and Prevention, 1998. Available at: *www.cdc.gov/ncidod/diseases/hepatitis /c/edu/1/default.htm.*

Gonorrhea

This is an inflammatory disease of the genital tract. Gonorrhea traditionally occurs on the genitals, but has recently appeared in the rectal region (as a result of anal sex) and in the throat (as a result of oral sex).

- Although easily treated by antibiotics, according to the CDC only "about 50 percent of men have some signs or symptoms," and "many women who are infected have no symptoms of infection."

    "Gonorrhea," Division of Sexually Transmitted Diseases, Centers For Disease Control and Prevention (September, 2000). Available at: *www.cdc.gov/nchstp/dstd/ Fact_Sheets/FactsGonorrhea.htm*

Untreated gonorrhea can have serious and permanent health consequences, including infertility damage to the prostate and urethra.

- The CDC reported "significant increases during 1994 to 1997 in rectal gonorrhea...among MSM," indicating that "safe sex" practices may not be taken as seriously as the AIDS epidemic begins to slow. In a follow-up report, the CDC stated that "gonorrhea rates in the United States increased by nine percent between 1997–1999...we have seen signs that gonorrhea is increasing among gay and bisexual men in a number of U.S. cities."

    "Increases in Unsafe Sex and Rectal Gonorrhea among Men Who Have Sex with Men—San Francisco, California, 1994–1997," 45; "CDC Issues Major New Report on STD Epidemics," Center for Disease Control Division of Sexually Transmitted Diseases (December 5, 2000).

- The incidence of throat Gonorrhea is strongly associated with homosexual behavior. The *Canadian Medical Association Journal* found that "gonorrhea was associated with urethral discharge... and homosexuality (3.7 times higher than the rate among heterosexuals)."

    J. Vincelette et al., "Predicators of Chlamydial Infection and Gonorrhea among Patients Seen by Private Practitioners," *Canadian Medical Association Journal* 144 (1995): 713–721.

- Similarly, a study in the *Journal of Clinical Pathology* found that homosexual men had a much higher prevalence of pharyngeal (throat) gonorrhea—15.2 percent compared with 4.1 percent for heterosexual men.

    SPR Jebakumar et al., "Value of Screeningfor Oropharyngeal Chlamydia Trachomatis Infection," *Journal of Clinical Pathology* 48 (1995): 658–661.

- "In addition to Alaska and New Hampshire, reported increases in gonorrhea and other STDs among MSM have been documented in other states, possibly as a result of an increase in unsafe sexual behavior related to the availability of highly active antiretroviral therapy."

"Gonorrhea—United States, 1998" *MMWR Weekly* 49 (June 23, 2000): 538–542.

Syphilis

This is a venereal disease that, if left untreated, can spread throughout the body over time, causing serious heart abnormalities, mental disorders, blindness, and death. The initial symptoms of syphilis are often mild and painless, leading some individuals to avoid seeking treatment.

- According to the National Institutes of Health, the disease may be mistaken for other common illnesses: "syphilis has sometimes been called 'the great imitator' because so many of the signs and symptoms are indistinguishable from those of other diseases." Early symptoms include rashes, moist warts in the groin area, slimy white patches in the mouth, or pus-filled bumps resembling chicken pox. According to the CDC, "transmission of the organism occurs during vaginal, anal, or oral sex."

"Some Facts about Syphilis," Division of Sexually Transmitted Diseases, Centers for Disease Control and Prevention, May 2001; "Syphilis Elimination: History in the Making," Division of Sexually Transmitted Diseases, Centers for Disease Control and Prevention (October 1999).

- In addition, the *Archives of Internal Medicine* found that homosexuals acquired syphilis at a rate ten times that of heterosexuals.

C. M. Hutchinson et al., "Characteristics of Patients with Syphilis Attending Baltimore STD Clinics," *Archives of Internal Medicine* 151 (1991): 511–516.

- The CDC reports that those who contract syphilis face potentially deadly health consequences: "It is now known that the genital sores caused by syphilis in adults also make it easier to transmit and acquire HIV infection sexually. There is a two to five fold increased risk of acquiring HIV infection when syphilis is present."

"Syphilis Elimination: History in the Making," Division of Sexually Transmitted Diseases, Centers for Disease Control and Prevention (October 1999).

- "While primary and secondary syphilis rates have declined almost

79

90 percent in the last decade, large outbreaks of syphilis have occurred in several U.S. cities among men who have sex with men (MSM). Data from these outbreak investigations and reports from behavioral surveys indicate that some MSM are participating in high-risk sexual behaviors that place them at increased risk for sexually transmitted diseases (STDs) and HIV infection. Similar findings have been reported internationally.

"Abstract 272 from the 2002 National STD Prevention Conference 'Changing Epidemiology of Syphilis and Other Sexually Transmitted Diseases Among Men Who Have Sex with Men'," National Center for HIV, STD and TB Prevention Division of Sexually Transmitted Diseases (March 5, 2002).

• "Because syphilis increases the likelihood of acquiring and transmitting HIV infection and because a large proportion of MSM with syphilis in these outbreaks are HIV positive, the rise in syphilis among MSM may indicate an increase in the incidence of HIV infection."

Ibid.

• *American Medical News* cites Ronald O. Valdiserri, MD, deputy director of CDC's National Center for HIV, STD and TB Prevention: "Syphilis outbreaks among gay and bisexual men, while a major concern in and of themselves, also signal the potential for a resurgence in HIV transmission." The reason, according to *American Medical News*, is that "since at least some of those men are also infected with the AIDS virus, public health officials fear that the transmission of the much more deadly disease could increase."

Susan J Landers, "Syphilis Rates Rise among Gays: Will Increases in HIV Follow?" *American Medical News* 45 (November 25, 2002): 29.

Gay Bowel Syndrome (GBS)

• The *Journal of the American Medical Association* refers to GBS problems such as proctitis, proctocolitis, and enteritis as "sexually transmitted gastrointestinal syndromes."

"STD Treatment Guidelines: Proctitis, Proctocolitis, and Enteritis," (Centers for Disease Control and Prevention) 1993. Homosexual advocates object to the use of this term (Gay Bowel Syndrome), which they say unfairly stigmatizes homosexual behavior. *Health Implications Associated with Homosexuality* (Austin: The Medical Institute for Sexual Health, 1999), 55.

- Many of the bacterial and protozoa pathogens that cause GBS are found in feces and transmitted to the digestive system: According to the pro-homosexual text *Anal Pleasure and Health*, "[s]exual activities provide many opportunities for tiny amounts of contaminated feces to find their way into the mouth of a sexual partner...The most direct route is oral-anal contact."

  Jack Morin, *Anal Pleasure and Health: A Guide for Men and Women* (San Francisco: Down There Press, 1998), 220.

- **Proctitis and Proctocolitis** are inflammations of the rectum and colon that cause pain, bloody rectal discharge and rectal spasms. Proctitis is associated with STDs such as gonorrhea, chlamydia, herpes, and syphilis that are widespread among homosexuals. The Sexually Transmitted Disease Information Center of the *Journal of the American Medical Association* reports that "[p]roctitis occurs predominantly among persons who participate in anal intercourse."

  Health Implications Associated with Homosexuality (Austin: The Medical Institute for Sexual Health, 1999), 55.

- **Enteritis** is inflammation of the small intestine. According to the Sexually Transmitted Disease Information Center of the *Journal of the American Medical Association*, "enteritis occurs among those whose sexual practices include oral-fecal contact."

  "STD Treatment Guidelines: Proctitis, Proctocolitis, and Enteritis."

- **Enteritis** can cause abdominal pain, severe cramping, intense diarrhea, fever, malabsorption of nutrients, or weight loss.

  Health Implications Associated with Homosexuality, 55. See also Jack Morin, *Anal Pleasure and Health: A Guide for Men and Women*, 220.

- According to a report in *The Health Implications of Homosexuality* by the Medical Institute for Sexual Health, some pathogens associated with enteritis and proctocolitis [see below] "appear only to be sexually transmitted among men who have sex with men."

  Health Implications Associated with Homosexuality, 55.

Kaposi Sarcoma (KS)

This is a relatively rare cancer in most populations, but it emerged as a common complication in people with AIDS. In fact, the American Cancer Society says:

- "It was in part the unusual and sudden appearance of this form of KS in so many young men at the start of the AIDS epidemic that led doctors to realize that a new disease had emerged."

  American Cancer Society, "What is Kaposi's Sarcoma?" *Cancer Reference Information*, online at: *http://www.cancer.org/docroot/cri/content/cri_2_4_1x_what_is_kaposis_sarcoma_21.asp?sitearea=cri* (accessed November 4, 2003).

- Kaposi sarcoma is caused by "Kaposi sarcoma-associated herpesvirus (KSHV), also know as human herpesvirus 8." Recent research in the *Journal of the American Medical Association* suggests that oral sex may be the primary means of transmission of KSHV. They reached this conclusion after noting that at points in the AIDS epidemic, "reductions in unprotected anal intercourse were accompanied by a decline in HIV prevalence but not in KSHV prevalence." Surveys of sexual behavior had shown, meanwhile, that "receptive oral intercourse with at least 1 partner without a condom was highly prevalent" among the homosexual men studied "throughout the 1984 through 1996 period, ranging between 60 percent and 90 percent of participants." The authors concluded, "Acquisition of KSHV via insertive penile-oral intercourse could explain the concentration of infection in homosexual men without ready spread to heterosexual groups."

  Dennis H. Osmond, et al., "Prevalence of Kaposi Sarcoma-Associated Herpresvirus Infection in Homosexual Men at Beginning of and During the HIV Epidemic," *Journal of the American Medical Association* 287, no. 2 (January 9, 2002), 224–25.

Homosexuals with STDs are at an increased risk for HIV infection

- The CDC reports: "Scientists know that the likelihood of both acquiring and spreading HIV is 2–5 times greater in people with STDs."

  "Need for Sustained HIV Prevention Among Men who Have Sex with Men," Divisions of HIV/AIDS Prevention, Centers for Disease Control (November 14, 2000).

- A CDC study attributed the high infection rate to having high numbers of anonymous sex partners: "[S]yphilis, gonorrhea, and chlamydia apparently have been introduced into a population of

MSM who have large numbers of anonymous partners, which can result in rapid and extensive transmission of STDs."

"Resurgent Bacterial Sexually Transmitted Disease among Men Who Have Sex with Men— King County, Washington, 1997–1999," Morbidity and Mortality Weekly Report: Centers for Disease Control (September 10, 1999), 773–777.

• The CDC report concluded: "Persons with STDs, including genital ulcer disease and nonulcerative STD, have a twofold to fivefold increased risk for HIV infection."

"Need for Sustained HIV Prevention Among Men who Have Sex with Men."

Anal cancer

• Homosexuals are at increased risk for this rare type of cancer, which is potentially fatal if the anal-rectal tumors metastasize to other bodily organs. Dr. Andrew Grulich calls "the rising rates of anal cancer the next great health threat to homosexual men."

Zmuda, "Rising Rates of Anal Cancer for Gay Men."

• Dr. Joel Palefsky, a leading expert in the field of anal cancer, reports that while the incidence of anal cancer in the United States is only 0.9/100,000, that number soars to 35/100,000 for homosexuals. That rate doubles again for those who are HIV positive, which, according to Dr. Palefsky, is "roughly ten times higher than the current rate of cervical cancer."

Bob Roehr, "Anal Cancer and You," *Between the Lines News* (November 16, 2000).

• At the Fourth International AIDS Malignancy Conference at the National Institutes of Health in May, 2000, Dr. Andrew Grulich announced that the incidence of anal cancer among homosexuals with HIV "was raised 37-fold compared with the general population."

"Studies Point to Increased Risks of Anal Cancer."

Lesbians are at risk through sex with MSM

• Many Lesbians also have had sex with men. The homosexual news-paper The *Washington Blade*, citing a 1998 study in the *Journal of*

Infectious Diseases, reported that "the study's data confirmed previous scientific observations that most women who have sex with women also have had sex with men. Among our subjects, sex with men was common, as were sexual practices between female partners that possibly could transmit HPV."

- The study added that "sex with men in the prior year was common, as were sexual practices between female partners that possibly could transmit HPV."

Rhonda Smith, "HPV Can be Transmitted between Women," *The Washington Blade* (December 4, 1998). Available at: *www.washblade.com/health/9901011h.*

High-risk sex with MSM endangers lesbians

- A study of sexually transmitted disease among lesbians reviewed in The *Washington Blade* notes: "Behavioral research also demonstrates that a woman's sexual identity is not an accurate predictor of behavior, with a large proportion of 'lesbian' women reporting sex with (often high risk) men."

Katherine Fethers et al., "Sexually Transmitted Infections and Risk Behaviors in Women Who Have Sex with Women," *Sexually Transmitted Infections* 76 (2000): 348.

- The study found that "the median number of lifetime male sexual partners was significantly greater for WSW (women who have sex with women) than controls (twelve partners versus six). WSW were significantly more likely to report more than 50 lifetime male sexual partners."

Ibid.

- A study in the *American Journal of Public Health* concurs that bisexual women are at increased risk for contracting sexually transmitted diseases: "Our findings corroborate the finding that WSMW (women who have sex with men and women) are more likely than WSMO (women who have sex with men only) to engage in various high-risk behaviors" and also "to engage in a greater number of risk-related behaviors." The study suggested that the willingness to engage in risky sexual practices "could be tied to a pattern of sensation-seeking behavior."

V. Gonzales, et al., "Sexual and Drug-Use Risk Factors for HIV and STDs: A Comparison of Women with and without Bisexual Experiences," *American Journal of Public Health* 89 (December 1999): 1846.

MSM spread HIV to women

- A five-year study by the CDC of 3,492 homosexuals aged fifteen to twenty-two found that one in six also had sex with women. Of those having sex with women, one-quarter "said they recently had unprotected sex with both men and women." Nearly 7 percent of the men in the study were HIV positive....The study confirms that young bisexual men are a 'bridge' for HIV transmission to women," said the CDC.

  "Bisexuals Serve as 'Bridge' Infecting Women with HIV."

"Exclusive" lesbian relationships also at risk

- The assumption that lesbians involved in exclusive sexual relationships are at reduced risk for sexual disease is false. The journal *Sexually Transmitted Infections* concludes: "The risk behavior profile of exclusive WSW was similar to all WSW." One reason for this is because lesbians "were significantly more likely to report past sexual contact with a homosexual or bisexual man and sexual contact with an IDU (intravenous drug user)."

  Fethers et al., "Sexually Transmitted Infections and Risk Behaviors in Women Who Have Sex with Women," 348.

Cancer risk factors for lesbians

- Citing a 1999 report released by the Institute of Medicine, an arm of the National Academy of Sciences, the homosexual newspaper The *Washington Blade* notes that "various studies on Lesbian health suggest that certain cancer risk factors occur with greater frequency in this population. These factors include higher rates of smoking, alcohol use, poor diet, and being overweight." Elsewhere the *Blade* also reports: "Some experts believe Lesbians might be more likely than women in general to develop breast or cervical cancer because a disproportionate number of them fall into high-risk categories."

  Rhonda Smith, "Childbirth Linked with Smaller Breast Tumor Size," *The Washington Blade* (December 17, 1999).

Sexually transmitted diseases among lesbians

- In a study of the medical records of 1,408 lesbians, the journal *Sexu-*

ally Transmitted Infections found that women who have sexual relations with women are at significantly higher risk for certain sexually transmitted diseases: "We demonstrated a higher prevalence of BV (bacterial vaginosis), hepatitis C, and HIV risk behaviors in WSW as compared with controls."

Fethers et al., "Sexually Transmitted Infections and Risk Behaviors in Women Who Have Sex with Women," 345.

Mental Health Problems

Compulsive behavior among lesbians

- A study published in *Nursing Research* found that "alcohol problem incidence in lesbians is estimated at 30 percent, three times the rate for United States women as a whole....Like most problem drinkers, 32 (91 percent) of the participants had abused other drugs as well as alcohol, and many reported compulsive difficulties with food (34 percent), codependency (29 percent), sex (11 percent), and money (6 percent)." In addition, "Forty-six percent had been heavy drinkers with frequent drunkenness."

Joanne Hall, "Lesbians Recovering from Alcoholic Problems: An Ethnographic Study of Health Care Expectations," *Nursing Research* 43 (1994): 238–244.

Alcohol abuse among homosexuals and lesbians

- A study of the health behaviors of 4,697 women in the *Archives of Family Medicine* found: "Lesbians and bisexual women were more likely than heterosexual women to consume alcohol more frequently and in larger quantities, and they were 5 times as likely to be classified as heavy drinkers."

Allison L. Diamant, et al, "Health Behaviors, Health Status, and Access to and Use of Health Care," *Archives of Family Medicine* 9 (November–December 2000): 1048.

- The *Journal of Consulting and Clinical Psychologists* reports that lesbian women consume alcohol more frequently, and in larger amounts, than heterosexual women. Lesbians were at significantly greater risk than heterosexual women for both binge drinking (19.4

percent compared to 11.7 percent), and for heavy drinking (7 percent compared to 2.7 percent).

Peter Freiberg, "Study: Alcohol Use More Prevelent for Lesbians," *The Washington Blade,* January 12, 2001, 21.

- Although the *Journal of Consulting and Clinical Psychologists* article found no significant connection between male homosexuals and alcohol abuse, a study in *Family Planning Perspective* concluded that male homosexuals were at greatly increased risk for alcoholism: "Among men, by far the most important risk group consisted of homosexual and bisexual men, who were more than nine times as likely as heterosexual men to have a history of problem drinking." The study noted that problem drinking may contribute to the "significantly higher STD rates among gay and bisexual men."

Karen Paige Erickson, Karen F. Trocki, "Sex, Alcohol and Sexually Transmitted Diseases: A National Survey," *Family Planning Perspectives* 26 (December 1994): 261.

High incidence of mental health problems among homosexuals and lesbians

A national survey of lesbians published in the Journal of Consulting and Clinical Psychology found that 75 percent of the nearly 2,000 respondents had pursued psychological counseling of some kind, many for treatment of long-term depression or sadness:

- "Among the sample as a whole, there was a distressingly high prevalence of life events and behaviors related to mental health problems. Thirty-seven percent had been physically abused and 32 percent had been raped or sexually attacked. Nineteen percent had been involved in incestuous relationships while growing up. Almost one-third used tobacco on a daily basis and about 30 percent drank alcohol more than once a week; 6 percent drank daily. One in five smoked marijuana more than once a month. Twenty-one percent of the sample had thoughts about suicide sometimes or often and 18 percent had actually tried to kill themselves....More than half had felt too nervous to accomplish ordinary activities at some time during the past year and over one-third had been depressed.

J. Bradford, et al., "National Lesbian Health Care Survey: Implications for Mental Health Care," *Journal of Consulting and Clinical Psychology* 62 (1994): 239, cited in *Health Implications Associated with Homosexuality*, 81.

Greater risk for suicide

- A study of 3,365 high school students published in Archives of Pediatric and Adolescent Medicine found: "Gay, lesbian, bisexual, or not sure male students were 6.50 times more likely to report a suicide attempt than heterosexual male students. Gay, lesbian, bisexual, or not sure female students were 2.02 times more likely to report a suicide attempt than their heterosexual female peers."

  Robert Garofalo, et al, "Sexual Orientation and Risk of Suicide Attempts among a Representative Sample of Youth," *Archives of Pediatric and Adolescent Medicine* 153 (May 1999): 490.

- The third National Health and Nutrition Examination Survey in *American Journal of Public Health* found that "homosexually experienced men are at greater risk for suicide symptoms" than heterosexual men: "In the current study, comparisons of homosexually experienced men with those reporting only opposite-sex sexual partners suggest that the former may be more than 5 times as likely to have attempted suicide."

  Susan D. Cochran, Vickie M. Mays, "Lifetime Prevalence of Suicide Symptoms and Affective Disorders among Men Reporting Same-sex Partners: Results from NHANES III" *American Journal of Public Health* 90 (April 2000): 576.

- A study that interviewed nearly 3,000 homosexual or bisexual men published in the *American Journal of Public Health* suggested a suicide rate for homosexual men that is three times the overall rate for U.S. males. The study authors found: "Twenty-one percent had made a suicide plan; 12 percent had attempted suicide (almost half of those 12 percent were multiple attempters). Most who attempted suicide made their first attempt before age 25."

  Jay P. Paul, et al, "Suicide Attempts among Gay and Bisexual Men: Lifetime Prevalence and Antecedents, *American Journal of Public Health* 92 (August 2002): 1338.

- A study of twins that examined the relationship between homosexuality and suicide, published in the *Archives of General Psychiatry*, found a substantially increased lifetime prevalence of suicidal symptoms in male twins reporting a same-gender sexual orientation (those with histories of same-gender partners in adulthood) compared with co-twins who report no same-gender partners." The homosexual twins were 6.5 times more likely than their twins to have attempted suicide."

  R. Herrell, et al., "A Co-Twin Study in Adult Men," *Archives of General Psychiatry* 56 (1999): 867.

- Another study published simultaneously in *Archives of General Psychiatry* followed 1,007 individuals from birth. Those classified as "gay, lesbian, or bisexual young people were at increased risks of major depression..., generalized anxiety disorder..., conduct disorder..., nicotine dependence..., other substance abuse and/or dependence..., multiple disorders..., suicidal ideation..., and suicide attempts."

D. Fergusson, et al., "Is Sexual Orientation Related to Mental Health Problems and Suicidality in Young People?" *Archives of General Psychiatry* 56 (October 1999), 876.

- Significantly, in his comments on the studies in the same issue of the journal, J. Michael Bailey cautioned against various speculative explanations of the results, such as the view that "widespread prejudice against homosexual people causes them to be unhappy or worse, mentally ill." According to Bailey, the question of whether "antihomosexual attitudes" were part of the explanation of suicidality among homosexual people "remains to be demonstrated."

J. Michael Bailey, "Homosexuality and Mental Illness," *Archives of General Psychiatry* 56 (October 1999), 883.

Reduced life span

A study published in the *International Journal of Epidemiology* on the mortality rates of homosexuals concluded that they have a significantly reduced life expectancy:

- "In a major Canadian centre, life expectancy at age twenty for gay and bisexual men is eight to twenty years less than for all men. If the same pattern of mortality were to continue, we estimate that nearly half of gay and bisexual men currently aged twenty years will not reach their sixty-fifth birthday. Under even the most liberal assumptions, gay and bisexual men in this urban centre are now experiencing a life expectancy similar to that experienced by all men in Canada in the year 1871."

Robert S. Hogg et al., "Modeling the Impact of HIV Disease on Mortality in Gay and Bisexual Men," *International Journal of Epidemiology* 26 (1997): 657.

Conclusion: In Their Own Words

Even a pro-homosexual organization such as the Gay and Lesbian Medical

Association (GLMA) cannot help but acknowledge the heightened health risks experienced by homosexuals. In twin press releases in 2002, the GLMA highlighted "ten things gay men should discuss" and "ten things lesbians should discuss with their health care providers." Yet they could just as easily have been labeled "top ten reasons why homosexuality is harmful to your health." Following are excerpts:

"Ten Things Gay Men Should Discuss with Their Health-Care Providers"

1. HIV/AIDS, Safe Sex

"That men who have sex with men are at an increased risk of HIV infection is well known," the article begins. It also notes that "the last few years have seen the return of many unsafe sex practices."

2. Substance Use

"Gay men use substances at a higher rate than the general population, and not just in larger communities such as New York, San Francisco, and Los Angeles. These include a number of substances ranging from amyl nitrate ('poppers'), to marijuana, Ecstasy, and amphetamines. The long-term effects of many of these substances are unknown; however current wisdom suggests potentially serious consequences as we age."

3. Depression/Anxiety

"Depression and anxiety appear to affect gay men at a higher rate than in the general population." The article adds, "Adolescents and young adults may be at particularly high risk of suicide because of these concerns."

4. Hepatitis Immunization

"Men who have sex with men are at an increased risk of sexually transmitted infection with the viruses that cause the serious condition of the liver known as hepatitis. These infections can be potentially fatal, and can lead to very serious long-term issues such as cirrhosis and liver cancer."

5. STDs

"Sexually transmitted diseases (STDs) occur in sexually active gay men at a high rate." The article notes that these include STD infections "for which no cure is available (HIV, Hepatitis A, B, or C virus, Human Papilloma Virus, etc.)."

6. Prostate, Testicular, and Colon Cancer

"Gay men may be at risk for death by prostate, testicular, or colon cancer."

7. Alcohol

"Although more recent studies have improved our understanding of alcohol use in the gay community, it is still thought that gay men have higher rates of alcohol dependence and abuse than straight men."

8. Tobacco

"Recent studies seem to support the notion that gay men use tobacco at much higher rates than straight men, reaching nearly 50 percent in several studies. Tobacco-related health problems include lung disease and lung cancer, heart disease, high blood pressure, and a whole host of other serious problems."

9. Fitness (Diet and Exercise)

"Problems with body image are more common among gay men than their straight counterparts, and gay men are much more likely to experience an eating disorder such as bulimia or anorexia nervosa." The article adds, "The use of substances such as anabolic steroids and certain supplements can adversely affect health. At the opposite end of the spectrum, overweight and obesity are problems that also affect a large subset of the gay community. This can cause a number of health problems, including diabetes, high blood pressure, and heart disease."

10. Anal Papilloma

"Of all the sexually transmitted infections gay men are at risk for, human papilloma virus—which cause anal and genital warts—is often thought to be little more than an unsightly inconvenience. However, these infections may play a role in the increased rates of anal cancers in gay men." The article also warns that "recurrences of the warts are very common, and the rate at which the infection can be spread between partners is very high."

Vincent M. B. Silenzio, MD, "Ten Things Gay Men Should Discuss with their Health Care Providers: Commentary," online at: *http://www.glma.org/news/releases/n02071710gaythings.html* (accessed November 4, 2003).

"Ten Things Lesbians Should Discuss with Their Health-Care Providers"

1. **Breast Cancer**
   "Lesbians have the richest concentration of risk factors for this cancer than [sic] any subset of women in the world."

2. **Depression/Anxiety**
   "Lesbians have been shown to experience chronic stress…" (The author attributes this to "homophobic discrimination," but offers no evidence to support that conclusion.)

3. **Gynecological Cancer**
   "Lesbians have higher risks for some of the gynecologic cancers."

4. **Fitness**
   "Research confirms that lesbians have higher body mass than heterosexual women. Obesity is associated with higher rates of heart disease, cancers, and premature death."

5. **Substance Use**
   "Research indicates that illicit drugs may be used more often among lesbians than heterosexual women."

6. **Tobacco**
   "Research also indicates that tobacco and smoking products may be used more often by lesbians than by heterosexual women. Whether smoking is used as a tension reducer or for social interactions, addiction often follows and is associated with higher rates of cancers, heart disease, and emphysema—the three major causes of death among all women."

7. **Alcohol**
   "Alcohol use and abuse may be higher among lesbians."

8. **Domestic Violence**
   "Domestic violence is reported to occur in about 11 percent of lesbian homes," the article states. It goes on to claim that this is "about half the rate of 20 percent reported by heterosexual women." However, this comparison fails to note that the highest rates of domestic violence among heterosexuals occur among those who are divorced,

separated, cohabiting, or in sexual relationships outside of marriage; *married* women experience the lowest rates of domestic violence of any household arrangement.

See Callie Marie Rennison, "Intimate Partner Violence and Age of Victim, 1993–99," *Bureau of Justice Statistics Special Report*, U.S. Department of Justice, Office of Justice Programs (revised November 28, 2001), 9–10.

9. Osteoporosis

"The rates and risks of osteoporosis among lesbians have not been well characterized yet."

10. Heart Health

"Smoking and obesity are the most prevalent risk factors for heart disease among lesbians," the article reports.

Katherine A. O'Hanlan, MD, "Ten Things Lesbians Should Discuss with their Health Care Providers: Commentary," online at: *http://www.glma.org/news/releases/n02071710lesbianthings.html* (accessed November 4, 2003).

CHAPTER 5

Do Homosexual Parents Pose Risks to Children?

A number of studies claim that children raised in gay and lesbian households fare no worse than those reared in traditional families. However, much of that research fails to meet acceptable standards for psychological research; it is compromised by methodological flaws and driven by political agendas. The deficiencies of studies on homosexual parenting include reliance upon an inadequate sample size, lack of random sampling, lack of anonymity of research participants, and self-presentation bias.

On the other hand, there is an abundance of evidence to demonstrate the dangerous consequences of homosexual behavior and the unstable nature of homosexual relationships. And despite the weaknesses of the research focused specifically on homosexual parents, there is significant evidence that their children suffer, particularly in the area of sexual adjustment.

Meanwhile, a well-established and growing body of evidence (amply documented in FRC's companion volume, *The Family Portrait*) shows that both mothers and fathers provide unique and irreplaceable contributions to the raising of children. Children reared in traditional families by a mother and father are happier, healthier, and more successful than children raised in non-traditional environments.

The claim: Children of homosexuals are "no different"

- Silverstein and Auerbach are examples of those who claim there is no essential difference between traditional mother-father families and homosexual-led families: "Other aspects of personal development and social relationships were also found to be within the normal range for children raised in lesbian and gay families." They suggest that "gay and lesbian parents can create a positive family context."

Louise B. Silverstein and Carl F. Auerbach, "Deconstructing the Essential Father," *American Psychologist* 54 (June 1999): 397–407.

- This conclusion is echoed in the official statement on homosexual parenting by the American Psychological Association's Public Interest Directorate, authored by openly lesbian activist Charlotte J. Patterson of the University of Virginia:

"In summary, there is no evidence that lesbians and gay men are unfit to be parents or that psychosocial development among children of gay men or lesbians is compromised in any respect....Not a single study has found children of gay or lesbian parents to be disadvantaged in any significant respect relative to children of heterosexual parents."

Charlotte J. Patterson, "Lesbian and Gay Parenting," *American Psychological Association Public Interest Directorate* (1995): 8.

This conclusion, however, is not as confident as it appears. In the next paragraph, Patterson qualifies her statement.

- Echoing Cramer's concern from a decade earlier, she writes: "It should be acknowledged that research on lesbian and gay parents and their children is still very new and relatively scarce....Longitudinal studies that follow lesbian and gay families over time are badly needed." The years have passed since Patterson's admission of the inadequacy of homosexual parenting studies, and we still await definitive, objective research substantiating her claims.

Ibid.

Weaknesses of Homosexual Parenting Studies

- Appearing in the *Journal of Counseling and Development*, a review of twenty studies on homosexual parenting found the following: "The generalizability of the studies is limited. Few studies employed control groups and most had small samples. Almost all parents were Anglo-American, middle class, and well educated. Measures for assessing gender roles in young children tend to focus on social behavior and generally are not accurate psychological instruments. Therefore it is impossible to make large scale generalizations...that would be applicable to all children."

David Cramer, "Gay Parents and Their Children: A Review of Research and Practical Implications," *Journal of Counseling and Development* 64 (April 1986): 506. See also Frederick W. Bozett, "Gay Fathers: A Review of the Literature," in *Homosexuality and the Family* (New York: Harrington Park Press, 1989), 152.

Homosexual parenting claims based on flawed research

* Patterson also acknowledges that "research in this area has presented a variety of methodological challenges," and that "questions have been raised with regard to sampling issues, statistical power, and other technical matters (e.g., Belcastro, Gramlich, Nicholson, Price, & Wilson, 1993)."

She adds, revealingly:

* "In addition, homosexual parenting research has been criticized for using poorly matched or no control groups in designs that call for such controls....Other criticisms have been that most studies have involved relatively small samples [and] that there have been inadequacies in assessment procedures employed in some studies."

Patterson, "Lesbian and Gay Parenting," 2.

Though she admits to serious methodological and design errors that would call into question the findings of any study, Patterson makes the astonishing claim that "even with all the questions and/or limitations that may characterize research in the area, none of the published research suggests conclusions different from those that will be summarized below." But any such conclusions are only as reliable as the evidence upon which they are based. If the alleged evidence is flawed, then the conclusions must likewise be considered suspect.

* In a study published in the *Journal of Divorce and Remarriage*, P. Belcastro et al. reviewed fourteen studies on homosexual parenting according to accepted scientific standards. Their "most impressive finding" was that "all of the studies lacked external validity. The conclusion that there are no significant differences in children raised by

lesbian mothers versus heterosexual mothers is not supported by the published research data base."

P. A. Belcastro et al., "A Review of Data Based Studies Addressing the Affects of Homosexual Parenting on Children's Sexual and Social Functioning," *Journal of Divorce and Remarriage* 20 (1993): 105, 106.

- Similarly, in their study of lesbian couples in *Family Relations*, L. Keopke et al. remark, "Conducting research in the gay community is fraught with methodological problems."

  L. Keopke et al., "Relationship Quality in a Sample of Lesbian Couples with Children and Child-free Lesbian Couples," *Family Relations* 41 (1992): 225.

A careful reading of studies used to lend support to homosexual parenting reveals more modest claims than are often attributed to them, as well as significant methodological limitations:

- "Nearly all of the existing studies of homosexual parenting have major deficiencies in sampling: They use a small sample size; they fail to obtain a truly representative sample due to sources of sampling bias; they do not use a random sample; or they use a sample with characteristics that are inappropriate for the crucial development research question involved in the study."

  J. Paul Guiliani and Dwight G. Duncan, "Brief of *Amici Curiae* Massachusetts Family Institute and National Association for the Research and Therapy of Homosexuality," Appeal to the Supreme Court of Vermont, Docket No. S1009-97CnC.

Inadequate sample size

Studies examining the effects of homosexual parenting are weakened by inordinately small sample sizes:

- After finding no significant difference between a group of nine children raised by lesbians and a similar group of children raised by heterosexual parents, S. L. Huggins admitted, "The meaning and implications of this finding are unclear, and the small sample size makes any interpretation of these data difficult."

  S. L. Huggins, "A Comparative Study of Self-esteem of Adolescent Children of Divorced Lesbian Mothers and Divorced Heterosexual Mothers," *Journal of Homosexuality* 18 (1989): 134.

- A report by J. M. Bailey et al. in *Developmental Psychology*, commenting on studies of the children of gay and lesbian parents, notes that "available studies [are] insufficiently large to generate much statistical power."

J. M. Bailey et al., "Sexual Orientation of Adult Sons of Gay Fathers," *Developmental Psychology* 31 (1995): 124.

• S. Golombok and F. Tasker admit in their follow-up study of children reared by lesbians, "It is possible that the small sample size resulted in an underestimate of the significance of group difference as a result of low statistical power (Type II error)."

Susan Golombok and Fiona L. Tasker, "Do Parents Influence the Sexual Orientation of Their Children? Findings from a Longitudinal Study of Lesbian Families," *Developmental Psychology* 32 (1996): 9.

• Elsewhere the same authors caution that negative effects of children reared by lesbians "could have remained undetected because of the relatively small sample size. Therefore, although discernible trends were identified, caution is required in interpreting these results."

Fiona L. Tasker and Susan Golombok, "Adults Raised as Children in Lesbian Families," *Developmental Psychology* 31 (1995): 213.

• In his study published in *Child Psychiatry and Human Development* comparing the children of homosexual and heterosexual mothers, G. A. Javaid frankly admits that "the numbers are too small in this study to draw any conclusions."

Ghazala A. Javaid, "The Children of Homosexual and Heterosexual Single Mothers," *Child Psychiatry and Human Development* 23 (1993): 245.

• J. Bigner and R. B. Jacobson state in the *Journal of Homosexuality*: "Those who do study gay fathers may be frustrated by the difficulties of obtaining valid and adequate sample sizes. Most often, researchers must deal with many methodological problems in locating and testing gay fathers in numbers sufficiently large to make acceptable statistical analyses of data. For this reason, what is known currently about gay fathers is weakened by these methodological problems. It is practically impossible to obtain a representative sample of gay fathers, and those studies published to date frequently utilize groups of white, urban, well-educated males for study because of convenience sampling."

Jerry J. Bigner and R. Brooke Jacobson, "Adult Responses to Child Behavior and Attitudes Toward Fathering: Gay and Nongay Fathers," *Journal of Homosexuality* 23 (1992): 99–112.

- In her study of lesbian families, Patterson admits to sampling bias: "Some concerns relevant to sampling issues should also be acknowledged. Most of the families who took part in the Bay Area Families Study were headed by lesbian mothers who were White, well educated, relatively affluent, and living in the greater San Francisco Bay Area. For these reasons, no claims about representativeness of the present sample can be made."

  Charlotte J. Patterson, "Families of the Lesbian Baby Boom: Parent's Division of Labor and Children's Adjustment," *Development Psychology* 31 (1995): 122.

- Similarly, N. L. Wyers, in his study of male and female homosexual parents that appeared in *Social Work*, acknowledges that his study "cannot be considered representative" and that "therefore, the findings cannot be generalized beyond the sample itself."

  Norman L. Wyers, "Homosexuality in the Family: Lesbian and Gay Spouses," *Social Work* 32 (1987): 144.

Lack of random sampling

Researchers use random sampling to ensure that the study participants are representative of the population being studied (for example, homosexuals or lesbians). Findings from unrepresentative samples have no legitimate generalization to the larger population.

- L. Lott-Whitehead and C. T. Tully admit the inherent weaknesses in their study of lesbian mothers: "This study was descriptive and, therefore, had inherent in its design methodological flaws consistent with other similar studies. Perhaps the most serious concerns representativeness....Probability random sampling...was impossible. This study does not purport to contain a representative sample, and thus generalizability cannot be assumed."

  Laura Lott-Whitehead and Carol T. Tully, "The Family Lives of Lesbian Mothers," *Smith College Studies in Social Work* 63 (1993): 265.

- L. Wyers acknowledges that he did not use random sampling procedures in his study of lesbian and gay spouses, rendering his study "vulnerable to all the problems associated with self-selected research participants."

  Wyers, "Homosexuality in the Family," 144.

- Golombok et al. write of their study: "A further objection to the findings lies in the nature of the samples studied. Both groups were volunteers obtained through gay and single-parent magazines and associations. Obviously these do not constitute random samples, and it is not possible to know what biases are involved in the method of sample selection."

Golombok et al., "Children in Lesbian and Single-parent Households: Psychosexual and Psychiatric Appraisal," *Journal of Child Psychology and Psychiatry* 24 (1983): 569.

Lack of anonymity of research participants

Research procedures guaranteeing complete anonymity are necessary to prevent a source of bias as to who will consent to participate as a research subject and ensure the truthfulness and candor of their answers.

- B. Harris and P. H. Turner point out in the *Journal of Homosexuality*: "Most gay/lesbian parents who participate in such research are concerned about their parenting and their children, and most have established a public gay identity. 'Closet' gay parents are difficult to identify, and their problems may be quite different from those of more openly gay parents."

Mary B. Harris and Pauline H. Turner, "Gay and Lesbian Parents," *Journal of Homosexuality* 12 (1985): 104.

- Harris and Turner employed superior research techniques to ensure the complete anonymity of their research subjects. As a result, in contrast to other studies, they reported problems associated with being a homosexual parent that had gone unreported by earlier studies: "Perhaps the anonymity of the present sampling procedure made subjects more willing to acknowledge those problems than those in earlier studies."

Harris and Turner, "Gay and Lesbian Parents," 112.

Self-presentation bias

A lack of random sampling and the absence of controls guaranteeing anonymity allow subjects to present a misleading picture to the researcher that conforms to the subject's attitudes or opinions and suppresses evidence that does not conform to the image he or she desires to present.

- In their National Lesbian Family Study, N. Gartrell et al. found that eighteen of nineteen studies of homosexual parents used a research procedure that was contaminated by self-presentation bias. Gartrell mentions the methodological problems of one longitudinal study of lesbian families: "Some may have volunteered for this project because they were motivated to demonstrate that lesbians were capable of producing healthy, happy children. To the extent that these subjects might wish to present themselves and their families in the best possible light, the study findings may be shaped by self-justification and self-presentation bias."

  Nanette Gartrell et al., "The National Lesbian Family Study: Interviews with Prospective Mothers," *American Journal of Orthopsychiatry* 66 (1996): 279.

- Harris and Turner admit, with regard to their study: "There is no way of knowing how representative the sample is.…The high proportion of gay subjects who indicated a willingness to be interviewed suggests that they were perhaps unusually interested in the issues raised in the questionnaire and thus willing to divulge their homosexuality to the researchers. Moreover, even though the questionnaire was anonymous, the gay parents may have been particularly biased toward emphasizing the positive aspects of their relationships with their children, feeling that the results might have implications for custody decisions in the future. Thus, all generalizations must be viewed with caution.…Because all uncorroborated self-report data are subject to biases, and because parents may deliberately or unconsciously minimize the extent of conflicts with their children, these findings cannot be accepted at face value."

  Harris and Turner, "Gay and Lesbian Parents," 111, 112.

Conclusion

In their thorough review of homosexual parenting studies, Robert Lerner and Althea K. Nagai found insufficient evidence to support the oft-repeated mantra that homosexual households are "just like" traditional families:

- "We conclude that the methods used in these studies are so flawed that these studies prove nothing. Therefore, they should not be used in legal cases to make any argument about 'homosexual vs. heterosexual' parenting. Their claims have no basis."

  Robert Lerner and Althea K. Nagai, *No Basis: What the Studies Don't Tell Us About Same Sex Parenting* (Washington: Ethics and Public Policy Center, 2001): 6.

Is the Homosexual Lifestyle Suitable for the Rearing of Children?

Homosexual relationships are characteristically unstable and are fundamentally incapable of providing children the security they need.

Homosexual promiscuity

Studies indicate that the average male homosexual has hundreds of sex partners in his lifetime.

- A. P. Bell and M. S. Weinberg, in their classic study of male and female homosexuality, found that 43 percent of white male homosexuals had sex with five hundred or more partners, with 28 percent having 1,000 or more sex partners.

  A. P. Bell and M. S. Weinberg, *Homosexualities: A Study of Diversity Among Men and Women* (New York: Simon and Schuster, 1978), 308, 309; See also A. P. Bell, M. S. Weinberg, and S. K. Hammersmith, *Sexual Preference* (Bloomington: Indiana University Press, 1981).

- In their study of the sexual profiles of 2,583 older homosexuals published in *Journal of Sex Research*, Paul Van de Ven et al. found that "the modal range for number of sexual partners ever [of homosexuals] was 101–500." In addition, 10.2 percent to 15.7 percent had between 501 and 1,000 partners. A further 10.2 percent to 15.7 percent reported having had more than 1,000 lifetime sexual partners.

  Paul Van de Ven et al., "A Comparative Demographic and Sexual Profile of Older Homosexually Active Men," *Journal of Sex Research* 34 (1997): 354.

- A survey conducted by the homosexual magazine *Genre* found that 24 percent of the respondents said they had had more than 100 sexual partners in their lifetime. The magazine noted that several respondents suggested including a category of those who had more than 1,000 sexual partners.

  "Sex Survey Results," *Genre* (October 1996), quoted in "Survey Finds 40 percent of Gay Men Have Had More Than 40 Sex Partners," *Lambda Report*, January 1998, 20.

- In his study of male homosexuality in *Western Sexuality: Practice and Precept in Past and Present Times*, M. Pollak found that "few homosexual relationships last longer than two years, with many men reporting hundreds of lifetime partners."

  M. Pollak, "Male Homosexuality," in *Western Sexuality: Practice and Precept in Past and Present*

Times, ed. P. Aries and A. Bejin, translated by Anthony Forster (New York, NY: B. Blackwell, 1985), 40–61, cited by Joseph Nicolosi in *Reparative Therapy of Male Homosexuality* (Northvale, New Jersey: Jason Aronson Inc., 1991), 124, 125.

Promiscuity among homosexual couples

Even in those homosexual relationships in which the partners consider themselves to be in a committed relationship, the meaning of "committed" typically means something radically different than in heterosexual marriage.

- In *The Male Couple,* authors David P. McWhirter and Andrew M. Mattison report that in a study of 156 males in homosexual relationships lasting from one to thirty-seven years: "Only seven couples have a totally exclusive sexual relationship, and these men all have been together for less than five years. Stated another way, all couples with a relationship lasting more than five years have incorporated some provision for outside sexual activity in their relationships."

  David P. McWhirter and Andrew M. Mattison, *The Male Couple: How Relationships Develop* (Englewood Cliffs: Prentice-Hall, 1984), 252, 253.

Most understood sexual relations outside the relationship to be the norm, and viewed adopting monogamous standards as an act of oppression.

- In *Male and Female Homosexuality,* M. Saghir and E. Robins found that the average male homosexual live-in relationship lasts between two and three years.

  M. Saghir and E. Robins, *Male and Female Homosexuality* (Baltimore: Williams & Wilkins, 1973), 225.

- In their *Journal of Sex Research* study of the sexual practices of older homosexual men, Paul Van de Ven et al. found that only 2.7 percent of older homosexuals had only one sexual partner in their lifetime.

  Van de Ven, et al., "A Comparative Demographic and Sexual Profile," 354.

- A study published in the journal *AIDS* in 2003 found that among homosexual men in the Netherlands, the "rate at which men with a steady partner acquire casual partners" averaged eight per year. Homosexual men without a "steady partner," on the other hand, were found to "acquire" an average of 22 casual sex partners per year.

  Maria Xiridou, et al., "The contribution of steady and casual partnerships to the incidence of HIV infection among homosexual men in Amsterdam," *AIDS* 17 (2003): 1031.

Are there any differences between homosexual 'couples' and heterosexual spouses?

The figures on homosexual promiscuity stand in stark contrast to the statistics regarding sexual fidelity within marriage:

- A nationally representative survey of 884 men and 1,288 women published in *Journal of Sex Research* found that 77 percent of married men and 88 percent of married women had remained faithful to their spouses.

    Michael W. Wiederman, "Extramarital Sex: Prevalence and Correlates in a National Survey," *Journal of Sex Research* 34 (1997): 170.

- In *The Social Organization of Sexuality: Sexual Practices in the United States*, E. O. Laumann et al. conducted a national survey that found that 75 percent of husbands and 85 percent of wives never had sexual relations outside of marriage.

    E. O. Laumann et al., *The Social Organization of Sexuality: Sexual Practices in the United States* (Chicago: University of Chicago Press, 1994), Table 5.15, 216.

- A telephone survey conducted for *Parade* magazine of 1,049 adults selected to represent the demographic characteristics of the United States found that 81 percent of married men and 85 percent of married women reported that they had remained faithful to their spouses.

    M. Clements, "Sex in America Today: A New National Survey Reveals How our Attitudes are Changing," *Parade*, August 7, 1994, pp. 4–6.

While the rate of fidelity within marriage cited by these studies remains far from ideal, there is a magnum order of difference between the negligible lifetime fidelity rate cited for homosexuals and the 75 to 88 percent cited for married couples.

Intimate partner violence within homosexual and lesbian relationships

Homosexual and lesbian relationships are far more violent than traditional married households:

- A study in the *Journal of Interpersonal Violence* examined conflict and violence in lesbian relationships. The researchers found that 90 percent of the lesbians surveyed had been recipients of one or more acts of verbal aggression from their intimate partners during the year prior to this study, with 31 percent reporting one or more incidents of physical abuse.

Lettie L. Lockhart et al., "Letting out the Secret: Violence in Lesbian Relationships," *Journal of Interpersonal Violence* 9 (1994): 469–492.

- In a survey of 1,099 lesbians, the *Journal of Social Service Research* found that "slightly more than half of the [lesbians] reported that they had been abused by a female lover/partner. The most frequently indicated forms of abuse were verbal/emotional/psychological abuse and combined physical-psychological abuse."

Gwat Yong Lie and Sabrina Gentlewarrier, "Intimate Violence in Lesbian Relationships: Discussion of Survey Findings and Practice Implications," *Journal of Social Service Research* 15 (1991): 41–59.

- In their book *Men Who Beat the Men Who Love Them: Battered Gay Men and Domestic Violence*, D. Island and P. Letellier postulate that "the incidence of domestic violence among gay men is nearly double that in the heterosexual population."

D. Island and P. Letellier, *Men Who Beat the Men Who Love Them: Battered Gay Men and Domestic Violence* (New York: Haworth Press, 1991), 14.

- A battering victimization study of 2,881 homosexuals published in the *American Journal of Public Health* found that "the 5-year prevalence of physical battering among urban MSM (22.0 percent) was significantly higher than either the annual prevalence of severe violence (3.4 percent) or the annual prevalence of total violence (11.6 percent) among a representative sample of women who were married or cohabiting with men....This study demonstrates that intimate partner abuse among urban MSM is a very serious public health problem."

Gregory L. Greenwood, et al, "Battering Victimization among a Probability-based Sample of Men Who Have Sex with Men," *American Journal of Public Health* 92 (December 2002): 1966–1967.

The low rate of intimate partner violence within marriage

A little-reported fact is that homosexual and lesbian relationships are far more violent than are traditional married households:

- The Bureau of Justice Statistics (U.S. Department of Justice) reports that married women in traditional families experience the lowest rate of violence compared with women in other types of relationships.

  "Violence Between Intimates," *Bureau of Justice Statistics Selected Findings*, November 1994, 2.

- A report by the Medical Institute for Sexual Health concurred: "It should be noted that most studies of family violence do not differentiate between married and unmarried partner status. Studies that do make these distinctions have found that marriage relationships tend to have the least intimate partner violence when compared to cohabiting or dating relationships."

  Health Implications Associated With Homosexuality (Austin: The Medical Institute for Sexual Health, 1999), 79.

Substance abuse among lesbians

- A study published in *Nursing Research* found that lesbians are three times more likely to abuse alcohol and to suffer from other compulsive behaviors: Like most problem drinkers, 32 (91 percent) of the participants had abused other drugs as well as alcohol, and many reported compulsive difficulties with food (34 percent), codependency (29 percent), sex (11 percent), and money (6 percent). Forty-six percent had been heavy drinkers with frequent drunkenness."

  Joanne Hall, "Lesbians Recovering from Alcoholic Problems: An Ethnographic Study of Health Care Expectations," *Nursing Research* 43 (1994): 238–244.

Difference in life expectancy between male homosexuals and heterosexuals

Another factor contributing to the instability of male homosexual households, which raises the possibility of major disruption for children raised in such households, is the significantly reduced life expectancy of male homosexuals.

- In chapter 6 of this booklet, a study in the *International Journal of Epidemiology* on the mortality rates of homosexuals is cited. The study concludes that the "life expectancy at age twenty for gay and bisexual men is eight to twenty years less than for all men."

  Robert S. Hogg et al., "Modeling the Impact of HIV Disease on Mortality in Gay and Bisexual Men," *International Journal of Epidemiology* 26 (1997): 657.

- In 1990, Wayne Tardiff and his partner, Allan Yoder, were the first homosexuals permitted to become adoptive parents in the state of New Jersey. Tardiff died in 1992 at age forty-four; Yoder died a few months later, leaving an orphaned five-year-old.

Obituaries, *The Washington Blade* (July 16, 1992): 23.

The Consequences for Children

Problems in social and academic adjustment

One significant study in an Australian journal has received too little attention in the American debate over homosexual parents. Sotirios Sarantakos, a sociologist, reported in the journal *Children Australia* on a study he conducted that avoided many of the pitfalls of most such studies.

- He compared "a sample of 174 primary school children living in three different types of families...58 children of heterosexual cohabiting couples, 58 children of heterosexual married couples and 58 children of homosexual (47 lesbian and 11 gay) couples," all of which included "at least one of their biological parents." The children were "matched according to age, gender, year of study, and parental characteristics (education, occupation, and employment status)."

Sotirios Sarantakos, "Children in three contexts: Family, education and social development," *Children Australia*, Vol. 21, No. 3, (1996), 23.

- The ratings of children's achievement in this study were "collected primarily from teachers and only secondarily from parents and children."

Ibid., 24

The author notes that this subjects the results to possible bias on the part of the teachers. (However, it *avoids* the risk of bias that comes from *self*-reporting on the part of homosexual parents and their children, who may have a vested interest in trying to show how successful they are.)

It should also be noted that all of the children in this study were being raised by *couples*, not by single parents. This does away with the argument that what is important for kids is having *two* parents (of any gender), rather than having a mother and a father specifically.

Sarantakos found that the children of married couples did the best, and the children of homosexual couples did the worst, in nine out of thirteen measures:

- Language

- Mathematics

- Sport

- Sociability

- Attitude to School and to Learning

- Parent-School Relationship

- Sex Identity (i.e., gender roles)

- School-Related Support (e.g., parents' help with homework)

- Parental Aspirations (for their children's education and career)

There were only three areas in which the children of homosexuals scored higher:

- Social Studies

- Personal Autonomy (of the child)

- Household Tasks (i.e., the contribution children make to them)

The report says "there were no statistically significant differences…regarding control and punishment of children."

Ibid., 24–28.

The author concludes:

- "Overall, the study has shown that children of married couples are more likely to do well at school, in academic and social terms, than children of cohabiting heterosexual and homosexual couples."

109

It's important to note that the author does *not* have an anti-homosexual agenda. In fact, he warns:

• "Before one jumps to conclusions encouraging homophobia and traditionalism, other relevant factors must be considered." Nevertheless, he states, "In this study, married couples seem to offer the best environment for a child's social and educational development."

Ibid., 29.

Sexual identity confusion among children raised in homosexual and lesbian households

There is growing evidence that children raised in such households headed by homosexuals are more likely to engage in sexual experimentation and in homosexual behavior.

• Studies indicate that 0.3 percent of all adult females report having practiced homosexual behavior in the past year, 0.4 percent have practiced homosexual behavior in the last five years, and 3 percent have ever practiced homosexual behavior in their lifetime.

A. M. Johnson et al., "Sexual Lifestyles and HIV Risk," *Nature* 360 (1992): 410–412; R. Turner, "Landmark French and British Studies Examine Sexual Behavior, including Multiple Partners, Homosexuality," *Family Planning Perspectives* 25 (1993): 91, 92.

• A study in *Developmental Psychology*, however, found that 12 percent of the children of lesbians became active lesbians themselves, a rate which is at least four times the base rate of lesbianism in the adult female population.

Tasker and Golombok, "Adults Raised as Children in Lesbian Families," 213.

• Numerous studies indicate that while nearly 5 percent of all males report having had a homosexual experience sometime in their lives, the number of exclusive homosexuals is considerably less: Between 1 and 2 percent of males report exclusive homosexual behavior over a several-year period (see Chapter 2).

ACSF Investigators, "AIDS and Sexual Behavior in France," *Nature* 360 (1992): 407–409; J. M. Bailey et al., "Sexual Orientation of Adult Sons of Gay Fathers," *Developmental Psychology* 31 (1995): 124–129; J. O. G. Billy et al., "The Sexual Behavior of Men in the United States," *Family Planning Perspectives* 25 (1993): 52–60; A. M. Johnson et al., "Sexual Lifestyles and HIV Risk," *Nature* 360 (1992): 410–412.

- However, J. M. Bailey et al. found that 9 percent of the adult sons of homosexual fathers were homosexual in their adult sexual behavior: "The rate of homosexuality in the sons (9 percent) is several times higher than that suggested by the population-based surveys and is consistent with a degree of father-to-son transmission."

Bailey et al., "Sexual Orientation of Adult Sons of Gay Fathers," 127–128.

- Even though they attempted to argue otherwise, Golombok and Tasker's study revealed in its results section a clear connection between being raised in a lesbian family and homosexuality: "With respect to actual involvement in same-gender sexual relationships, there was a significant difference between groups....None of the children from heterosexual families had experienced a lesbian or gay relationship." By contrast, five (29 percent) of the seventeen daughters and one (13 percent) of the eight sons in homosexual families reported having at least one same-sex relationship.

Tasker and Golombok, "Do Parents Influence the Sexual Orientation?" 7.

- R. Green et al. writing in *Archives of Sexual Behavior*, reported that the few experimental studies that included even modestly larger samples (13–30) of boys or girls reared by homosexual parents found "developmentally important statistically significant differences between children reared by homosexual parents compared to heterosexual parents. For example, children raised by homosexuals were found to have greater parental encouragement for cross-gender behavior [and] greater amounts of cross-dressing and cross-gender play/role behavior."

Richard Green et al., "Lesbian Mothers and Their Children: A Comparison with Solo Parent Heterosexual Mothers and Their Children," *Archives of Sexual Behavior* 15 (1986): 167–184.

- In the *American Sociological Review*, authors Judith Stacey and Timothy J. Biblarz alluded to the "political incorrectness" of their finding of higher rates of homosexuality among children raised in homosexual households: "We recognize the political dangers of pointing out that recent studies indicate that a higher proportion of children of lesbigay parents are themselves apt to engage in homosexual activity."

Judith Stacey and Timothy J. Biblarz, "(How) Does the Sexual Orientation of Parents Matter," *American Sociological Review* 66 (2001): 174, 179.

- Stacy and Biblarz also reported "some fascinating findings on the number of sexual partners children report," including: "The adolescent and young adult girls raised by lesbian mothers appear to have been more sexually adventurous and less chaste....In other words, once again, children (especially girls) raised by lesbians appear to depart from traditional gender-based norms, while children raised by heterosexual mothers appear to conform to them."

Stacey and Biblarz, Ibid.

Greater incidence of incest in homosexual parent families

- A study in *Adolescence* found: "A disproportionate percentage—29 percent—of the adult children of homosexual parents had been specifically subjected to sexual molestation by that homosexual parent, compared to only 0.6 percent of adult children of heterosexual parents having reported sexual relations with their parent....Having a homosexual parent(s) appears to increase the risk of incest with a parent by a factor of about 50."

P. Cameron and K. Cameron, "Homosexual Parents," *Adolescence* 31 (1996): 772.

Anecdotal evidence

Although anecdotal evidence alone cannot prove definitively the existence of specific trends in the lives of children with homosexual parents, it is often employed in news stories that extol the virtues of some specific homosexual couple and the love between them and the children they are raising. However, one rarely hears such stories balanced by the personal testimonies of children traumatized by the same experience. Yet there are many such children, as demonstrated by a remarkable pro-homosexual book titled *Different Mothers: Sons and Daughters of Lesbians Talk About Their Lives.* Despite the oft-repeated claim of "no difference," the editor of this collection of first-hand accounts admits:

- "Their lives, both their emotional lives and public lives, are affected by our lifestyles."

Louise Rafkin, editor, *Different Mothers: Sons and Daughters of Lesbians Talk About Their Lives* (Pittsburgh: Cleis Press, 1990), 10.

Following are a number of excerpts from this book, with the names and ages of the writer. While most of these people end up defending their lesbian mothers, much of the trauma they have experienced is still evident in their candid reflections:

- Kyneret Hope (25 years old)

  "I experienced [lesbian] separatism as a constant level of anger and negativity....That was part of the lifestyle I knew, but there was also a down side: men were called mutants, straight women were considered disowned sisters who wasted woman-energy on men, and other lesbians were sometimes accused of being government spies sent to infiltrate and undermine the community. Anyone who was not like us was evil, and I had to be careful not to cross over to the enemy's camp."

  Kyneret Hope, "Of Lesbian Descent," in *Different Mothers: Sons and Daughters of Lesbians Talk About Their Lives*, 59.

- Michael (27 years old)

  "Lesbians should not fill their children with their own fears and hatreds. I say this after considering the causes of needless pain in my past, and my troubles understanding the present....I do recall our wishing our mothers were more attentive to us than to each other. We kids would get together and have sex, males or females in any combination—unbeknownst to our parents, but ironically I don't think any of us really knew what our mothers' lesbianism really meant....Since my parents had sex with the same sex (my mother with other women, my stepfather with me), I had not understood that homosexuality was wrong. Also, at the time I couldn't figure out my own sexuality because I was having sex with people of both sexes....Until I was sixteen or so, I was sexually abused by many straight men [sic], 'friends' of my mother's whom I was occasionally left with. I wondered, what was going on on this planet? The end result of all of this abuse is that today I don't trust people. Period.... Lesbians who hate or fear men take this out on boy children. I suspect that the same thing might happen with gay fathers and girl children."

  "Out of the Pain," in *Different Mothers: Sons and Daughters of Lesbians Talk About Their Lives*, 110–116.

- Carla Tomaso (grew up in the 1950s)

  "I've been angry with my mother all my life. The fact that she kept boundaries between me and her sexual experiences with women when I was a child made me feel that she was choosing others over me, that I wasn't important. It also probably sexualized her for me in an inappropriate way....But I don't seem to have problems with being a lesbian myself....In fact, I think my mother showed me that lesbianism is a possibility..."

Carla Tomaso, "I'm Always Looking for My Mother," in *Different Mothers: Sons and Daughters of Lesbians Talk About Their Lives*, 140–41.

• Kathlean Hill (20 years old)

"I just remember thinking that all lesbians felt the same way my mother felt about everything. If that were true, then all lesbians would talk about men as crude, destructive, dishonest, sleazy creatures that were really not supposed to exist. They were a mistake. Yet while she told me these things, she also taught me to question authority. I began my questioning right about there; I chose not to believe her. At this point I already thought lesbianism meant treating men as inferior. From there I decided that lesbians were a bunch of hypocritical women. Just a bunch of women who preach freedom and individuality, yet their values and beliefs were basically homogeneous. So, at a very young age, lesbianism looked like a bleak future to me. Terre called my sister and me 'baby dykes,' making us wear these small hand-crafted lesbian signs she had made for us by a local lesbian jeweler. Both my sister, Maureen, and I have always been extremely resentful of that. It always seemed so unfair to label a child's sexuality so young."

Kathlean Hill, "Change and Consistency," in *Different Mothers: Sons and Daughters of Lesbians Talk About Their Lives*, 150.

• Carey Conley (21 years old)

"I built up a great deal of fear and frustration. I was angry that I was not part of a 'normal' family and could not live with a 'normal' mother. I wondered what I did to deserve this. Why did my biological mother let a lesbian adopt me? How could she think that this life was better than what she could have given me?...During these years I talked with my sister about my feelings and problems. We discussed how we didn't understand my mother and her lifestyle. We talked of how we resented her for placing us in such a situation, all the while knowing how hard it would be for us."

Carey Conley, "Always Changes" in *Different Mothers: Sons and Daughters of Lesbians Talk About Their Lives*, 157–59.

• Adam Levy (23 years old)

"I have always had an accelerated knowledge of sexual education due to the nature of my mother's and her first lover's occupations. They were both physical and sex education teachers for the Board of Education in New York City....I think the combination of my knowledge, coupled with the feeling that there are no rules about sexual behavior, may make it appear to some that I enjoy variety when it comes to women. The reality is that I am in no hurry to find a lifetime mate; therefore I find myself always looking for new possibilities....Meanwhile, I made up my own rules. Rules which I created out of the freedom allowed me by my parents, especially that of my mother's sexual preference. When mom broke the big rule—the one that says only men and women get married—I began to question other rules which had designs on my life."

Adam Levy, "Mom Breaks the Big Rule," in *Different Mothers: Sons and Daughters of Lesbians Talk About Their Lives*, 163–64.

Even more poignant are the comments by some of the youngest children of lesbian parents:

- **Katie and Tessa O'Neal (10 and 13 years old)**
  "We have talked about how some gay women dress like men and how some men dress like women. I think that is really weird, and I don't understand why they do it. I think it must be really hard on their kids, too."

  Katie and Tessa O'Neal, "A Real Big Secret," in *Different Mothers: Sons and Daughters of Lesbians Talk About Their Lives*, 40.

- **Zea (13 years old)**
  "I don't have many men in my life, so I'm not as comfortable around them as I would like to be."

  "Like Sisters," in *Different Mothers: Sons and Daughters of Lesbians Talk About Their Lives*, 124.

- **Guilemere (5 years old)**
  "Some friends ask me questions about my moms, and I get embarrassed and scared to answer. And sometimes mad that I don't have brothers and sisters. I really want more kids in our family....Once I told Aunt Shari and mommy to get married to men and have babies. Then they could tell the men to live in another state!"

  "Making Family," in *Different Mothers: Sons and Daughters of Lesbians Talk About Their Lives*, 130.

- **Lovenia (9 years old)**

  "Once in a while I wish my dad was in my life, because I never knew him as my father....Sometimes I talk to my mother about it, and I have told her that she has made my life difficult."

  "It Just Happens to Be," in *Different Mothers: Sons and Daughters of Lesbians Talk About Their Lives*, 142–44.

Jakii Edwards was raised by a lesbian mother and has written an entire book about it. She summarizes the experiences of such children this way:

- "We constantly wonder if we will eventually become gay. There is humiliation when other kids see our parents kissing a same-sex lover in front of us. Trust me, it's hard on the children, no matter how much they love their gay parent. The homosexual community may never admit it, but the damage stemming from their actions can be profound."

  Jakii Edwards with Nancy Kurrack, *Like Mother, Like Daughter? The effects of growing up in a homosexual home* (Vienna, VA: Xulon Press, 2001), 8.

A Political Agenda: Redefining Marriage and Family

It is not the intention of homosexual activists simply to make it possible for homosexuals and lesbians to partake of conventional married life. By their own admission they aim to change the essential character of marriage, removing precisely the aspects of fidelity and chastity that promote stability in the relationship and the home:

- Paula Ettelbrick, former legal director of the Lambda Legal Defense and Education Fund, has stated, "Being queer is more than setting up house, sleeping with a person of the same gender, and seeking state approval for doing so....Being queer means pushing the parameters of sex, sexuality, and family, and in the process transforming the very fabric of society."

  Paula Ettelbrick, quoted in William B. Rubenstein, "Since When Is Marriage a Path to Liberation?" *Lesbians, Gay Men, and the Law,* (New York: The New Press, 1993), 398, 400.

- Homosexual writer and activist Michelangelo Signorile goes so far as to redefine the term *monogamy*: For these men the term "monogamy" simply doesn't necessarily mean sexual exclusivity....The term "open relationship" has for a great many gay men come to have one specific definition: A relationship in which the partners have sex on the outside often, put away their resentment and jealousy, and discuss their outside sex with each other, or share sex partners.

Michelangelo Signorile, *Life Outside* (New York: HarperCollins, 1997), 213.

- The views of Signorile and Ettelbrick regarding marriage are widespread in the homosexual community. According to the *Mendola Report*, a mere 26 percent of homosexuals believe that commitment is most important in a marriage relationship.

Mary Mendola, *The Mendola Report* (New York: Crown, 1980), 53.

- Former homosexual William Aaron explains why even homosexuals involved in "committed" relationships do not practice monogamy: In the gay life, fidelity is almost impossible. Since part of the compulsion of homosexuality seems to be a need on the part of the homophile to "absorb" masculinity from his sexual partners, he must be constantly on the lookout for [new partners]. Consequently the most successful homophile "marriages" are those where there is an arrangement between the two to have affairs on the side while maintaining the semblance of permanence in their living arrangement.

William Aaron, *Straight* (New York: Bantam Books, 1972), 208, cited by Joseph Nicolosi in *Reparative Therapy of Male Homosexuality*, 125, quoted by Robert H. Knight in "How Domestic Partnerships and 'Gay Marriage' Threaten the Family," Family Research Council, *Insight* (June 1994), 9.

Supporters of homosexual "families" raise questions about their suitability for children

- In their study in *Family Relations*, L. Koepke et al. observed, "Even individuals who believe that same-sex relationships are a legitimate choice for adults may feel that children will suffer from being reared in such families."

Koepke, et al., "Relationship Quality in a Sample of Lesbian Couples with Children and Child-free Lesbian Couples," 228.

- Writing in the *Journal of Homosexuality*, J. J. Bigner and R. B. Jacobson describe the homosexual father as "socioculturally unique," trying to take on "two apparently opposing roles: that of a father (with all its usual connotations) and that of a homosexual man."

117

They describe the homosexual father as "both structurally and psychologically at social odds with his interest in keeping one foot in both worlds: parenting and homosexuality."

Bigner and Jacobson, "Adult Responses to Child Behavior and Attitudes Toward Fathering," 174, 175.

Children really need a mom and a dad

The importance of the traditional family has been increasingly verified by research showing that children from married two-parent households do better academically, financially, emotionally, and behaviorally. Meanwhile, they also experience much lower rates of many social pathologies, including:

- premarital childbearing;

  Kristin A. Moore, "Nonmarital School-Age Motherhood: Family, Individual, and School Characteristics," *Journal of Adolescent Research* 13 (October 1998), 433–457.

- illicit drug use;

  John P. Hoffman and Robert A. Johnson, "A National Portrait of Family Structure and Adolescent Drug Use," *Journal of Marriage and the Family* 60 (August 1998), 633–645.

- arrest;

  Chris Coughlin and Samuel Vucinich, "Family Experience in Preadolescence and the Development of Male Delinquency," *Journal of Marriage and the Family* 58 (May 1996), 491–501.

- health, emotional, or behavioral problems;

  Deborah A. Dawson, "Family Structure and Children's Health and Well-Being: Data from the 1988 National Health Interview Survey on Child Health," *Journal of Marriage and the Family* 53 (August 1991), 573–584.

- poverty;

  Federal Interagency Forum on Child and Family Statistics, *America's Children: Key Indicators of Well-Being 2001*, Washington, D.C., 14.

- or school failure or expulsion.

  (Dawson, op.cit.).

- These benefits are then passed on to future generations as well, because children raised by married parents are themselves less likely to cohabit or to divorce as adults.

Paul R. Amato and Alan Booth, *A Generation at Risk: Growing Up in an Era of Family Upheaval,* Cambridge, Massachusetts: Harvard University Press, 1997, 111–115.

These benefits do not arise simply from having two adult caretakers. Children have a specific need for both a mother and a father.

- Blankenhorn discusses the different but necessary roles that mothers and fathers play in children's lives: "If mothers are likely to devote special attention to their children's present physical and emotional needs, fathers are likely to devote special attention to their character traits necessary for the future, especially qualities such as independence, self-reliance, and the willingness to test limits and take risks."

- Blankenhorn further explains: "For the child, from the beginning, the mother's love is an unquestioned source of comfort and the foundation of human attachment. But the father's love is almost a bit farther away, more distant and contingent. Compared to the mother's love, the father's must frequently be sought after, deserved, earned through achievement.

David Blankenhorn, *Fatherless America* (New York: Basic Books, 1995), 219.

Author and sociologist David Popenoe confirms that mothers and fathers fulfill different roles in their children's lives.

- In *Life without Father* Popenoe notes, "Through their play, as well as in their other child-rearing activities, fathers tend to stress competition, challenge, initiative, risk taking and independence. Mothers in their care-taking roles, in contrast, stress emotional security and personal safety."

- Parents also discipline their children differently: "While mothers provide an important flexibility and sympathy in their discipline, fathers provide ultimate predictability and consistency. Both dimensions are critical for an efficient, balanced, and humane child-rearing regime."

David Popenoe, *Life Without Father* (Cambridge: Harvard University Press, 1996), 144, 146.

In his analysis of human cultures, the eminent Harvard sociologist Pitirim Sorokin argued that no society has ceased to honor the institution of marriage and survived. Sorokin considered traditional marriage and parenting as the fulfillment of life's meaning for both individuals and society:

- "Enjoying the marital union in its infinite richness, parents freely fulfill many other paramount tasks. They maintain the procreation of the human race. Through their progeny they determine the hereditary and acquired characteristics of future generations. Through marriage they achieve a social immortality of their own, of their ancestors, and of their particular groups and community. This immortality is secured through the transmission of their name and values, and of their traditions and ways of life to their children, grandchildren, and later generations."

Pitirim Sorokin, *The American Sex Revolution* (Boston: Porter Sargent Publishers, 1956), 6, 77–105.

CHAPTER 6

Is There a Link Between Homosexuality and Child Sexual Abuse?

Even people who remain apathetic about homosexual behavior among adults may have concerns about the impact of homosexuality on children. There is concern that pro-homosexual teaching in schools may undermine parental values and even encourage questioning youngsters to prematurely label themselves as "gay" (see the Family Research Council's *Family Policy* on "Homosexuality and Children," Vol. 15, No. 5, Nov.–Dec. 2002). There is concern that homosexuals do not provide an acceptable role model to children as teachers, mentors, and especially as parents (see Chapter 5).

But perhaps most alarming is the fear that homosexuals are more likely to engage in child sexual abuse. This fear was highlighted by the scandal which dominated the headlines in 2002, during which the American public learned at the same time that many children (mostly boys) had been molested by Catholic priests, and that a surprising number of priests may be homosexual in orientation.

Despite efforts by homosexual activists to distance the gay lifestyle from pedophilia, there remains a disturbing connection between the two. This is because, by definition, male homosexuals are sexually attracted to other males. While many homosexuals may not seek young sexual partners, the evidence indicates that disproportionate numbers of gay men seek adolescent males or boys as sexual partners. In this chapter we will consider the following evidence linking homosexuality to pedophilia:

- Pedophiles are invariably males: Almost all sex crimes against children are committed by men.

- Homosexuals are overrepresented in child sex offenses: Individuals from the 1 to 3 percent of the population that is sexually attracted to the same sex are committing up to one-third of the sex crimes against children.

- Some homosexual activists defend the historic connection between homosexuality and pedophilia: Such activists consider the defense of "boy-lovers" to be a legitimate gay-rights issue.

- Pedophile themes abound in homosexual literary culture: Gay fiction as well as serious academic treatises promote "intergenerational intimacy."

Male Homosexuals Commit a Disproportionate Number of Child Sex Abuse Cases

Homosexual apologists admit that some homosexuals sexually molest children, but they deny that homosexuals are more likely to commit such offenses. After all, they argue, the majority of child molestation cases are heterosexual in nature. While this is correct in terms of absolute numbers, this argument ignores the fact that homosexuals comprise only a very small percentage of the population.

The evidence indicates that homosexual men molest boys at rates grossly disproportionate to the rates at which heterosexual men molest girls.

To demonstrate this it is necessary to connect several statistics related to the problem of child sex abuse: 1) men are almost always the perpetrator; 2) up to one-third or more of child sex abuse cases are committed against boys; 3) less than three percent of the population are homosexuals. Thus, a tiny percentage of the population (homosexual men), commit one-third or more of the cases of child sexual molestation.

Men account for almost all sexual abuse of children cases

- An essay on adult sex offenders in the book *Sexual Offending Against Children* reported: "It is widely believed that the vast majority of sexual abuse is perpetrated by males and that female sex offenders only account for a tiny proportion of offences. Indeed, with 3,000 adult male sex offenders in prison in England and Wales at any one time, the corresponding figure for female sex offenders is 12!"

Dawn Fisher, "Adult Sex Offenders: Who are They? Why and How Do They Do It?" in Tony Morrison, et al., eds., *Sexual Offending Against Children* (London: Routledge, 1994), 11.

• Kee MacFarlane, et al., writing in *Sexual Abuse of Young Children: Evaluation and Treatment* report: "The large majority of sexual per-petrators appear to be males (Herman & Hirschman, 1981; Lind-holm & Willey, 1983)."

Kee MacFarlane, et al., *Sexual Abuse of Young Children: Evaluation and Treatment* (New York: The Guilford Press, 1986), 9.

• A report by the American Professional Society on the Abuse of Children states: "In both clinical and non-clinical samples, the vast majority of offenders are male."

John Briere, et al., eds., *The APSAC Handbook on Child Maltreatment* (Thousand Oaks, California: Sage Publications, 1996), 52, 53.

• A study in the *Journal of Sex Research* states that "pedophilia does not exist, or is extremely rare, in women."

Kurt Freund, et al., "Pedophilia and Heterosexuality vs. Homosexuality," *Journal of Sex & Marital Therapy* 10 (Fall 1984): 198; See also Freund, K, and Watson, R. J., "The Proportions of Het-erosexual and Homosexual Paedophiles among Sex Offenders against Children: an Exploratory Study," *Journal of Sex and Marital Therapy* 18 (1992): 34.

A significant percentage of child sexual abuse victims are boys

• According to the *Journal of Child Psychiatry*: "It was commonly believed fifteen years ago that girls were abused in excess of boys in a ratio of about 9 to 1, but contemporary studies now indicate that the ratio of girls to boys abused has narrowed remarkably....The majority of community studies suggest a...ratio...in the order of 2 to 4 girls to 1 boy."

Bill Watkins & Arnon Bentovim, "The Sexual Abuse of Male Children and Adolescents: A Review of Current Research," *Journal of Child Psychiatry* 33 (1992); in Byrgen Finkelman, *Sexual Abuse* (New York: Garland Publishing, 1995), 300.

• Another study found that "some authors now believe that boys may be sexually abused as commonly as girls (Groth, 1978; O'Brien, 1980)."

MacFarlane, *Sexual Abuse of Young Children: Evaluation and Treatment*, 9.

- A study of 457 male sex offenders against children in *Journal of Sex & Marital Therapy* found that "approximately one-third of these sexual offenders directed their sexual activity against males."

Kurt Freund, et al., "Pedophilia and Heterosexuality vs. Homosexuality," *Journal of Sex & Marital Therapy* 10 (1984): 197. "The proportional prevalence of offenders against male children in this group of 457 offenders against children was 36 percent." See also, Kurt Freund, et al., "Heterosexuality, Homosexuality, and Erotic Age Preference," "Approximately one-third of these individuals had victimized boys and two-thirds had victimized girls. This finding is consistent with the proportions reported in two earlier studies," 107.

- Sexual abuse of boys is underreported: The actual percentage of child sexual abuse victims who are boys very likely exceeds the above estimates. Many researchers echo the view of the *Journal of Child Psychiatry* study, which refers to the "under-reporting of the incidence and prevalence of sexual abuse in boys."

Watkins & Bentovim, "The Sexual Abuse of Male Children and Adolescents," 315.

- Dr. Robert Johnson, in *Medical Aspects of Human Sexuality*, reports: "The vast majority of cases of male sexual molestation is not reported. As a result, these young men keep both the incidents and their feelings to themselves."

Robert L. Johnson, "Long-term Effects of Sexual Abuse in Boys," *Medical Aspects of Human Sexuality* (September 1988): 38.

- The Department of Justice report on child sexual exploitation explains why the percentage of boy victims is underestimated: "Adolescent boy victims are highly likely to deny certain types of sexual activity.…They are embarrassed and ashamed of their behavior and rightfully believe that society will not understand their victimization.…No matter what the investigator does, most adolescent boys will deny they were victims."

"Understanding and Investigating Child Sexual Exploitation," (U.S. Department of Justice, Office of Justice Programs, 1997), 12.

- The *Journal of Child Psychiatry* adds: "Boys are usually encultured into an ethos where self-reliance, independence and sexual prowess are valued, while showing hurt or homosexuality are denigrated.… This may lead to powerful repression or deletion of the experience, with failure to report."

Watkins & Bentovim, "The Sexual Abuse of Male Children and Adolescents," 302

Homosexuals comprise less than 3 percent of the population

- Relying upon three large data sets: the General Social Survey, the National Health and Social Life Survey, and the U.S. census, a recent study in *Demography* estimates the number of exclusive male homosexuals in the general population at 2.5 percent, and the number of exclusive lesbians at 1.4 percent.

  Dan Black, et al., "Demographics of the Gay and Lesbian Population in the United States: Evidence from Available Systematic Data Sources," *Demography* 37 (May 2000): 141.

- Similarly, *Archives of Sexual Behavior* reports that a large population study of 7,076 persons in the Netherlands found the following: "Of the men who were sexually active in the preceeding year, 2.8 percent (n = 82) had had sex with male partners...Of women who were sexually active in the preceding year, 1.4 percent (n = 43) had had sex with female partners.

  Theodorus G. M. Sandfort, et al., "Same-Sex Sexuality and Quality of Life: Findings from the Netherlands Mental Health Survey and Incidence," Study *Archives of Sexual Behavior* 32 (February, 2003):16.

- A study of the sexual behavior of men in the United States based on the National Survey of Men (a nationally representative sample comprised of 3,321 men aged twenty to thirty-nine, published in *Family Planning Perspectives)*, found that "2 percent of sexually active men aged twenty to thirty-nine...had had any same-gender sexual activity during the last ten years. Approximately 1 percent of the men (1.3 percent among whites and 0.2 percent among blacks) reported having had exclusively homosexual activity.

  John O. G. Billy, et al., "The Sexual Behavior of Men in the United States," *Family Planning Perspectives* 25 (March/April 1993): 58.

- In a survey of studies on homosexuals in different populations, the *Archives of Sexual Behavior* reported a random sample of Hawaii State residents interviewed by telephone. The study found "just about 3 percent of males and 1.2 percent of females as having engaged in same-sex or bisexual activity." However, this relatively higher number is attributed to the fact that the study was not limited to exclusive homosexuals, but included all those who at some time in their lives engaged in same-sex activities.

  Milton Diamond, "Homosexuality and Bisexuality in Different Populations," *Archives of Sexual Behavior* 22 (1993): 300. Significantly, a number of studies that were surveyed, and which skewed the overall percentages of homosexuals upwards, included such vague definers as those having had "any homosexual body contact." In contrast, one study that was limited to self-identifying homosexuals found that less than 2 percent of the male respondents considered their "sexual orientation" to be homosexual, 293.

For more information, see Chapter 2 ("How Many Homosexuals Are There?").

Homosexual pedophiles are vastly overrepresented in child sex abuse cases

Homosexual pedophiles sexually molest children at a far greater rate compared to the percentage of homosexuals in the general population.

- A study in the *Journal of Sex Research* found, as we have noted above, that "approximately one-third of [child sex offenders] had victimized boys and two-thirds had victimized girls." The authors then make a prescient observation: "*Interestingly, this ratio differs substantially from the ratio of gynephiles (men who erotically prefer physically mature females) to androphiles (men who erotically prefer physically mature males), which is at least 20 to 1.*"

  Freund, "Heterosexuality, Homosexuality, and Erotic Age Preference," p. 107. In this and previous studies, Freund claims that homosexuals are no more likely than heterosexuals to be attracted to children (p. 115). However, Silverthorn, et al., mentions the limitations of studies by Freund and others: "Studies of homosexual male preferences are also limited....The Freund et al. (1973) study was possibly compromised because the homosexual men used in the study were selected to be sexually attracted to adults, but not teenaged, males. The Bailey et al. (1994) study was limited in that it did not present participants with objective stimuli but simply asked participants to report what age of sexual partner they preferred...the Jankowiak et al. (1992) study...was limited in two ways: the homosexual male participants had a limited age range of 'middle-aged professionals' and the stimuli presented to participants were also of a limited age range ('university to middle-aged')." Silverthorn attempted to correct these deficiencies, and in his study found that homosexuals "preferred younger partners than those who preferred female partners"—including those as young as fifteen. Zebulon A. Silverthorne & Vernon L. Quinsey, "Sexual Partner Age Preferences of Homosexual and Heterosexual Men and Women," *Archives of Sexual Behavior* 29 (February 2000): 67–76.

In other words, although heterosexuals outnumber homosexuals by a ratio of at least 20 to 1, homosexual pedophiles commit about one-third of the total number of child sex offenses.

Similarly, the *Archives of Sexual Behavior* also noted that homosexual pedophiles are significantly overrepresented in child sex offense cases:

- The best epidemiological evidence indicates that only 2 to 4 percent of men attracted to adults prefer men (ACSF Investigators, 1992;

Billy et al., 1993; Fay et al., 1989; Johnson et al., 1992); in contrast, around 25 to 40 percent of men attracted to children prefer boys (Blanchard et al., 1999; Gebhard et al., 1965; Mohr et al., 1964). *Thus, the rate of homosexual attraction is 6 to 20 times higher among pedophiles.*

Ray Blanchard, et al., "Fraternal Birth Order and Sexual Orientation in Pedophiles," *Archives of Sexual Behavior* 29 (2000): 464.

- The stark imbalance between homosexual and heterosexual child molestations was confirmed in the *Archives of Sexual Behavior* study itself, which divided 260 pedophile participants into three groups: "152 heterosexual pedophiles (men with offenses or self-reported attractions involving girls only), 43 bisexual pedophiles (boys and girls), and 65 homosexual pedophiles (boys only)." In other words, 25 percent of the offenders were homosexual pedophiles—or 41 percent if those who molest girls as well as boys are included.

Ibid.

Other studies report an unusually high percentage of child molestations by homosexual pedophiles:

- A study on pedophilia in the *Psychiatric Journal of the University of Ottawa* reported: "According to the literature, findings of a two-to-one ratio of heterosexual to homosexual pedophiles have been documented."

John M. W. Bradford, et al., "The Heterogeneity/Homogeneity of Pedophilia," *Psychiatric Journal of the University of Ottawa* 13 (1988): 225. Elsewhere the study notes: "Researchers have variously estimated the incidence of homosexual pedophilia between 19 percent and 33 percent of reported molestations," 218.

- The *Journal of Sex Research* reports a study that included "199 offenders against female children and 96 offenders against male children....This would indicate a proportional prevalence of 32 percent of homosexual offenders against children."

Freund, "Pedophilia and Heterosexuality vs. Homosexuality," 197.

- A study of male child sex offenders in *Child Abuse and Neglect* found that fourteen percent targeted only males, and a further 28 percent chose males as well as females as victims, thus indicating that 42 percent of male pedophiles engaged in homosexual molestation.

Michele Elliott, "Child Sexual Abuse Prevention: What Offenders Tell Us," *Child Abuse and Neglect* 19 (1995): 581.

Are Men Who Molest Boys Really "Homosexuals?"

As demonstrated above, child sexual abuse which is homosexual in nature (that is, involving a perpetrator and victim of the same sex) occurs at rates far in excess of the rate of consenting homosexual relations between adults. Even pro-homosexual activists do not attempt to dispute this fact.

Instead, they downplay its significance by arguing that pedophiles who engage in homosexual child abuse are not actually "homosexual" in their sexual attractions to adults. In other words, they argue in effect that "homosexuality" and "pedophilia" are each distinct "sexual orientations" unto themselves, with no overlap between the two. It is this rationale that explains how a homosexual advocacy organization, the Human Rights Campaign, can publish a "Fact Sheet on Sexual Orientation and Child Abuse" that states: "A sexual abuser who molests a child of the same sex is usually not considered homosexual."

However, this sharp distinction between homosexuality and pedophilia is not found in the scholarly literature.

"Homosexual pedophiles": a clinical term

The fact is, however, that the terms "homosexual" and "pedophile" are not mutually exclusive: they describe two intersecting types of sexual attraction. *Webster's Dictionary* defines "homosexual" as someone who is sexually attracted to persons of the same sex. "Pedophile" is defined as "an adult who is sexually attracted to young children." The former definition refers to the *gender* of the desired sexual object, while the latter refers to the *age* of the desired sexual object.

A male "homosexual pedophile," then, is defined as someone who is generally (but not exclusively, see below) sexually attracted to boys, while a female "homosexual pedophile" is sexually attracted to girls. Although homosexual activists would have us believe that "pedophiles" are simply attracted to children in general, without any preference as to their sex, that is not what the scholarly literature shows.

- The term "homosexual pedophile" was first used in the early twentieth century by the Viennese psychiatrist Dr. Richard von Krafft-Ebing, who pioneered the systematic study of sexual deviance.

Krafft-Ebing described pedophiles as heterosexually, homosexually, or bisexually oriented.

Bradford, "The Heterogeneity/Homogeneity of Pedophilia," 218.

• This division has been accepted by pedophiles themselves. A publication by the London Paedophilic Informational Exchange states: "[Pedophiles] can be of either sex or any [sexual] orientation, i.e., homosexual, heterosexual or bisexual."

Paedophilia: Some Questions and Answers (London: Paedophilic Informational Exchange, 1978); quoted in Seth L. Goldstein, "Investigating Child Sexual Exploitation: Law Enforcement's Role," *FBI Law Enforcement Bulletin* 53 (January 1984): 23.

The distinction between homosexual and heterosexual pedophiles is well attested in the scholarly literature:

• A study of pedophiles in *Behavior Research and Therapy* concluded: "The second, and perhaps the most important observation we made, is that a homosexual and a heterosexual subgroup can be delineated among these offenders....Categorizing them in this way revealed important differences in the pattern of their sexual preferences."

W. L. Marshall, et al., "Sexual Offenders against Male Children: Sexual Preferences," *Behavior Research and Therapy* 26 (March 1988): 390.

• The *Journal of Sex & Marital Therapy* published a study on the same topic, which discussed "the proportional prevalences of heterosexual and homosexual pedophilia." The study commented on a study that found that "the percentage of the homosexual pedophiles would be 45.8." Even adjusted downward for exhibitionists, "this would still indicate a much higher percentage (34 percent) of homosexuals among pedophiles than among men who prefer physically mature partners."

Freund, "Pedophilia and Heterosexuality vs. Homosexuality," 194, 197.

• In a review of studies on pedophilia, the *Psychiatric Journal of the University of Ottawa* concluded: "The findings of previous studies report that pedophiles can be divided into heterosexual and homosexual pedophiles according to their erotic preference....This was confirmed in this recent study." The article classified homosexual pedophilia into three types: the socially inadequate homosexual pedophile, the intrusive homosexual pedophile, and the undifferentiated homosexual pedophile.

Bradford, "The Heterogeneity/Homogeneity of Pedophilia," 217–219.

- The *International Journal of Offender Therapy and Comparative Criminology* refers to homosexual pedophiles as a "distinct group." The victims of homosexual pedophiles "were more likely to be strangers, that they were more likely to have engaged in paraphiliac behavior separate from that involved in the offence, and that they were more likely to have past convictions for sexual offences....Other studies [showed a] greater risk of reoffending than those who had offended against girls" and that the "recidivism rate for male-victim offenders is approximately twice that for female-victim offenders."

  James Bickley and Anthony R. Beech, "Classifying Child Abusers: Its Relevance to Theory and Clinical Practice," *International Journal of Offender Therapy and Comparative Criminology* 45 (2001): 56.

Homosexuals and homosexual pedophiles engage in a wide variety of sexual behavior

Despite this evidence, in their efforts to divorce homosexuality from pedophilia, homosexual apologists insist on a rigid, narrow definition of the terms "homosexual" and "pedophile" that permits no overlap of the terms. They deny that homosexuals are attracted in inordinate numbers to boys. They also claim that pedophiles cannot be classified as "homosexual" if at any time they have had sexual relations with women.

- Pro-homosexual activists rest much of this argument on a single study by Carole Jenny, et al., which claims that only 2 of 269 child molesters could be identified as gay or lesbian. However, the Jenny study utilized an atypical research technique: The reported child molesters themselves were not interviewed. Instead, the researchers relied upon the subjective reports of "informants" who accompanied the child-victim to the medical clinic. Only if the "informant" explicitly volunteered the opinion that perpetrator was a homosexual, and that opinion was recorded on the clinic's medical chart, was he or she classified as such. Moreover, if there was any evidence that the perpetrator had ever engaged in a heterosexual relationship, he or she was automatically classified as heterosexual. The Jenny study used this narrow profile despite the fact that the study itself found that 22 percent of the children had been molested by a person of the same sex. In these cases the molesters clearly engaged in homosexual sexual molestation.

Carole Jenny, et al., "Are Children at Risk for Sexual Abuse by Homosexuals?" *Pediatrics* 94 (July 1994): 41–44.

However, such a narrow definition does not do justice to the complex nature of pedophilia. Researchers have long been aware that pedophiles exhibit a wide variety of sexual attractions and behavior.

- A study on sex offenders in the *International Journal of Offender Therapy and Comparative Criminology* notes that "the reason child sexual abusers are successful at remaining undetected is because they do not fit a stereotype."

  Krisin A. Danni, et al., "An Analysis of Predicators of Child Sex Offender Types Using Presentence Investigation Reports," *International Journal of Offender Therapy and Comparative Criminology* 44 (2000): 491.

The data indicates that homosexuality and pedophilia are intersecting categories that admit to a wide variety of sexual behavior. For example:

Homosexual males are sexually attracted to underage boys

- A study in *Archives of Sexual Behavior* found that homosexual men are attracted to young males. The study compared the sexual age preferences of heterosexual men, heterosexual women, homosexual men, and lesbians. The results showed that, in marked contrast to the other three categories, "all but 9 of the 48 homosexual men preferred the youngest two male age categories," which included males as young as age fifteen.

  Zebulon A. Silverthorne & Vernon L. Quinsey, "Sexual Partner Age Preferences of Homosexual and Heterosexual Men and Women," 73.

- In *The Gay Report*, by homosexual researchers Karla Jay and Allen Young, the authors report data showing that 73 percent of homosexuals surveyed had at some time had sex with boys sixteen to nineteen years of age or younger."

  Karla Jay and Allen Young, *The Gay Report: Lesbians and Gay Men Speak Out about Sexual Experiences and Lifestyles* (New York: Summit Books, 1979), 275.

Homosexual pedophiles are often attracted to adult males

- A study of sex offenders against male children in *Behavior Research and Therapy* found that male homosexual pedophiles are sexually attracted to "males of all ages." Compared to non-offenders, the offenders showed "greater arousal" to slides of nude males as old as twenty-four: "As a group, the child molesters responsed [sp] with moderate sexual arousal...to the nude males of all ages."

  Marshall, "Sexual Offenders against Male Children: Sexual Preferences," 383.

- A study of Canadians imprisoned for pedophilia in the *Journal of Interpersonal Violence* noted that some of the adult male offenders engaged in homosexual acts with adult males.

  W. L. Marshall, et al., "Early Onset and Deviant Sexuality in Child Molesters," *Journal of Interpersonal Violence* 6 (1991): 323–336.

- Many pedophiles, in fact, consider themselves to be homosexual. A study of 229 convicted child molesters in *Archives of Sexual Behavior* found that "86 percent of offenders against males described themselves as homosexual or bisexual."

  W. D. Erickson, "Behavior Patterns of Child Molesters," *Archives of Sexual Behavior* 17 (1988): 83.

- Fr. John Harvey, founder and director of Courage, a support ministry for Catholics who struggle with same-sex attraction, explains that "the pedophile differs from the ordinary homosexual in that the former admires *boyishness* in the object of his affections, while the latter admires manliness." However, the categories are not completely separate: "While granting that the majority of homosexuals are not aroused by young boys, the distinction between homosexuality and homosexual pedophilia is not quite absolute. In some cases the interest oscillates between young adolescents and adults, in others between boys and adolescents; in exceptional cases a man may be interested in boys at one time and adults at another."

  John F. Harvey, O.S.F.S., *The Homosexual Person: New Thinking in Pastoral Care* (San Francisco: Ignatius Press: 1987): 221.

Many pedophiles are attracted to women, marry, and have children

Gay activists insist that pedophilia has nothing to do with homosexuality because pedophiles are only sexually interested in children, whereas homosexuals only have sexual relations with adults. We have already seen that this stereotypical view is not correct with regard to homosexuals. There is also abundant evidence demonstrating that, while primarily interested in children, pedophiles nevertheless exhibit a wide variety of sexual behaviors, including relationships with women:

- A study in *Child Abuse and Neglect* found that 48 percent of the offenders either were married or had been married at some time.

  Elliott, "Child Sexual Abuse Prevention: What Offenders Tell Us," 581.

- The *Journal of Interpersonal Violence* studied the sexual preferences of male pedophiles who sexually abused children. When they compared the sexual response of the pedophiles with the control group, they found, unexpectedly: "Surprisingly, the two groups did not differ in their response to the nude female stimuli."

  Marshall, "Sexual Offenders against Male Children: Sexual Preferences," 383.

- A study in the *Psychiatric Journal of the University of Ottawa* reported that "most of the middle-aged pedophiles have had significant adult sexual activity." Fifty-eight percent of the pedophiles in one study had at least one child, while other research indicated that "more than two-thirds of the married pedophiles in their sample had children, with an average of two to three children per subject."

  Bradford, "The Heterogeneity/Homogeneity of Pedophilia," 219, 224.

- A report by the Department of Justice addressed the devious strategems of pedophiles, who will go to great lengths to conceal their true desires: "Preferential sex offenders may be 'pillars of the community' and are often described as 'nice guys.' They almost always have a means of access to children (for example, through marriage, neighborhood, or occupation.)"

  "Understanding and Investigating Child Sexual Exploitation," 5.

Many homosexuals have also engaged in heterosexual relationships

- The National Health and Social Life Survey found that while 4.9 percent of American men have engaged in some homosexual activity since age 18 and 2.0 percent identify their sexual orientation as homosexual, only 0.6 percent of them have engaged exclusively in homosexual activity since puberty. In other words, at least 70 percent of self-identified homosexual men have also engaged in heterosexual relationships. An additional 0.8 percent of American men explicitly identify themselves as bisexual. (See Chapter 2)

Edward O. Laumann, John H. Gagnon, Robert T. Michael, and Stuart Michaels, *The Social Organization of Sexuality: Sexual Practices in the United States* (Chicago: The University of Chicago Press, 1994), 294–96, 310–312.

- The *Boston Globe* reported that in the first three years of Vermont's legally-recognized "civil unions" for homosexual couples, nearly 40 percent of the 5,700 homosexual couples who have obtained civil unions include at least one partner who used to be married.

Patricia Wen, "A Civil Tradition: Data Show Same-Sex Unions in Vt. Draw a Privileged Group," *The Boston Globe*, June 29, 2003, B1.

- Pro-homosexual sociologist Judith Stacey notes, "Most contemporary lesbian and gay parents procreated within heterosexual marriages." Ironically, when the issue is something homosexuals want to promote (like "gay parents") rather than something they want to deny (like homosexual child abuse), homosexual activists use a very expansive definition of who is homosexual. Stacey and her colleague Timothy Biblarz note that inflated estimates of the number of children being raised by homosexual parents, which are often put forward by homosexual activists, depend upon "classifying as a lesbigay parent anyone who reports that even the idea of homoerotic sex is appealing," even if they are in a heterosexual relationship or marriage.

Judith Stacey and Timothy J. Biblarz, "(How) Does the Sexual Orientation of Parents Matter," *American Sociological Review* 66 (2001): 165.

Thus, the evidence shows one cannot assume that pedophiles are not attracted to adults, nor can one assume that homosexuals will not have heterosexual relationships or even marriages. Therefore, homosexual pedophiles cannot be narrowly defined as individuals who are solely attracted to underage boys. In fact there is considerable overlap between homosexuality and pedophilia.

Pedophilia in Gay Culture

There exists a disturbing historical connection between pedophilia and the gay-rights movement

- David Thorstad is a homosexual activist and historian of the gay-rights movement. He is a former president of New York's Gay Activists Alliance (GAA), a prototype activist group founded in December 1969. The GAA at its inception opposed age of consent laws, which prohibited adults from having sex with children. Thorstad is also a pedophile and founding member of the North American Man/Boy Love Association (NAMBLA).

Thorstad is co-author, with John Lauritsen, of *The early homosexual rights movement (1864–1935)* (New York: Times Change Press, 1974). For GAA's position regarding age-of-consent laws, see: David Thorstad, "May/Boy Love and the American Gay Movement" *Journal of Homosexuality* 20 (1990): 252.

- Thorstad argues that there is a natural and undeniable connection between homosexuality and pedophilia. He expresses bitterness that the gay rights movement has, in his view, abandoned pedophilia. Thorstad writes: "Boy-lovers were involved in the gay movement from the beginning, and their presence was tolerated. Gay youth groups encouraged adults to attend their dances....There was a mood of tolerance, even joy at discovering the myriad of lifestyles within the gay and lesbian subculture."

Ibid., 253.

- In the early years there was some reluctance to accept pedophilia, primarily among feminist and lesbian activist groups. In March 1979 the Lesbian Feminist Liberation (LFL) accusing "so-called Man/Boy Lovers" of "attempting to legitimize sex between children and adults....Feminists easily recognize this as the latest attempt to make palatable the sexual exploitation of children." The coalition went on record as opposing "the sexual abuse of children by heterosexual or homosexual persons."

Ibid., 258.

- Despite this opposition, Thorstad claims that by 1985 homosexual pedophiles had won acceptance within the gay movement. He cites Jim Kepner, then curator of the International Gay and Lesbian Archives in Los Angeles: "A point I've been trying to make is that if we reject the boylovers in our midst today we'd better stop waving the banner of the Ancient Greeks, of Michelangelo, Leonardo da Vinci, Oscar Wilde, Walt Whitman, Horatio Alger, and Shakespeare. We'd better stop claiming them as part of our heritage unless we are broadening our concept of what it means to be gay today."

Ibid., 266.

ILGA and NAMBLA: An unseemly connection

In 1985, the notorious pro-pedophile organization NAMBLA (North American Man/Boy Love Association) was admitted as a member in New York's council of Lesbian and Gay Organizations as well as the International Gay Association—now the International Lesbian and Gay Association (ILGA). In the mid-1990's ILGA's association with NAMBLA and other pedophile groups cost the organization its status as a Non-Governmental Organization in the United Nations.

ILGA's renewed attempt to gain admittance to the UN was rejected again in April 2002 because the organization "did not document that it had purged pedophile groups such as [NAMBLA]." The *Washington Times* reports that Ishtiag H. Anrabi, Pakistani delegate to the UN Economic and Social Council, expressed concern that ILGA was continuing to be secretive about ties with pedophile groups: "For more than a year, the ILGA has refused to provide documentation or allow review of its membership list to demonstrate that pedophilia groups have been expelled."

George Archibald, "U.N. Group Keeps Ban on Gay Lobby," *Washington Times* (May 1, 2002).

Pedophile themes abound in gay literature

The late "beat" poet Allen Ginsberg illustrates the seamless connection between homosexuality and pedophilia. Many know Ginsberg as an illustrious "out" homosexual poet: fewer are aware that he was also a pedophile.

- Biographer Raymond-Jean Frontain refers to Ginsberg's publications in both NAMBLA Bulletin and NAMBLA Journal. He discusses how Ginsberg's biographers failed to discuss his poems that contained pederastic themes: "Although both Shumacher and Barry Miles (Ginsberg's initial biographer) frankly discuss Ginsberg's sexual politics, neither refers to his involvement with the controversial North American Man/Boy Love Association....I reread Collected Poems and Ginsberg's two subsequent collections, surprised by the pattern of references to anal intercourse and to pederasty that emerged."

Raymond-Jean Frontain, "The Works of Allen Ginsberg," *Journal of Homosexuality* 34 (1997): 109.

Ginsberg was one of the first of a growing number of homosexual writers who cater to the fascination with pedophilia in the gay community.

- Mary Eberstadt, writing in the *Weekly Standard*, documents how the taboo against sex with children continues to erode—with the impetus coming from homosexual writers. Revealingly, the examples Eberstadt provides of pedophilia in current literature come from gay fiction. Eberstadt cites the *Village Voice*, which states that "Gay fiction is rich with idyllic accounts of 'intergenerational relationships,' as such affairs are respectfully called these days."

Mary Eberstadt, "'Pedophilia Chic' Reconsidered" *The Weekly Standard* 6 (January 8, 2001).

Other examples of pedophilia-themed gay fiction:

- In the introduction of the "mainstream" homosexual anthology *Penguin Book on International Gay Writing,* David Leavitt notes matter-of-factly that "Another 'forbidden' topic from which European writers seem less likely to shrink is the love of older men for young boys." Leavitt praises one book with a pedophilic theme included in the anthology as a "coolly assured narrative [which] compels the reader to imagine the world from a perspective he might ordinarily condemn."

Ibid., p. 22.

- Several texts included in another anthology, *The Gay Canon: Great Books Every Gay Man Should Read,* feature scenes of man-boy sex. One such book is praised as "an operatic adventure into the realms of love, personality, ambition and art…a pure joy to read." The protagonist is "a pedophile's dream: the mind of a man in the body of a boy." Another novel which includes graphic descriptions of sexual violence against boys is said to "[tear] straight to the heart of one of the greatest sources, community-wide, of 1990's gay angst: What to do with men who love boys?"

Ibid.

- Yet another anthology of homosexual fiction, *A History of Gay Literature: The Male Tradition,* published by Yale University Press, includes "a longish chapter on 'Boys and Boyhood' which is a seemingly definitive account of pro-pedophile literary works." The author appears more concerned with the feelings and emotions of the man than with his boy victim. He explores the question of "whether or not you regard [having sex with boys] as a way of retreating from life or, on the contrary, *as a way of engaging with it at its most honest and least corrupted level.*"

Ibid., 23. Emphasis added by Eberstadt.

137

A significant percentage of books that have appeared on the Gay Men's Press fiction bestseller list contain pedophilia themes, including:

- *Some Boys:* described as a "memoir of a lover of boys" that "evokes the author's young friends across four decades."

  Ibid., 23.

- *For a Lost Soldier:* the story of a sexual relationship between a soldier and an eleven-year-old boy, set during World War II.

  Ibid.

- *A Good Start, Considering:* yet another story about an eleven-year-old boy (!) who suffers sexual abuse but is rescued by a teenager who "offers him love and affection"

  From the Gay Men's Press website: *www.gmppubs.co.uk/cgi-bin/web_store/web_store.cgi*

- *Terre Haute:* billed as "A poetic novel of sexual awakening in the American Midwest, tracing an adolescent's journey from introspection to perilous desire."

  Ibid.

- *Shiva and Arun:* the story of two Indian adolescents who "discover early on the joys of sex."

  Ibid.

- *Teardrops on My Drum:* barefoot kids in 1920s' Liverpool search for "adventure, love and sex."

  Ibid.

Pro-pedophilia publications

Recent years have seen the appearance of publications that lend a scholarly veneer to the fascination with pedophilia in the gay community. Such publications attempt to make the case for "intergenerational intimacy." The nation's largest gay publisher, Alyson Publications, which distributes *Daddy's Roommate* and other homosexual books that promote homosexuality to children, publishes books advocating man-boy sex, including:

- *Paedophilia: The Radical Case,* which contains detailed information on how to engage in sexual relations with young boys.

  Tom O'Carroll, *Paedophilia: The Radical Case* (Boston: Alyson Publications, 1982).

- *The Age Taboo,* another defense of pedophilia which claims: "Boy-lovers…are not child molesters. The child abusers are…parents who force their staid morality onto the young people in their custody."

  Daniel Tsang, editor, *The Age Taboo: Gay Male Sexuality, Power, and Consent* (Boston: Alyson Publications; London: Gay Men's Press, 1981), 144.

The *Journal of Homosexuality* and Pedophilia

The *Journal of Homosexuality* is viewed as the premier "mainstream" English-language publication of the gay movement. One prominent editor is John DeCecco, a psychologist at San Francisco State University who also serves on the editorial board of the Dutch pedophile journal *Paidika*. It is therefore not surprising to see pedophilia promoted on its pages:

- In 1990 the *Journal of Homosexuality* published a series of essays on pedophilia that were eventually published as *Male Intergenerational Intimacy: Historical, Socio-Psychological, and Legal Perspectives*, edited by pedophile Edward Brongersma. None of the essays offered any substantive criticism of pedophilia: Most blatantly promoted man-boy love as the natural right of homosexuals.

  Theo Sandfort, Edward Brongersma, Alex van Naerssen, editors, *Male intergenerational intimacy : historical, socio-psychological, and legal perspectives* (New York : Haworth Press, 1991).

- In 1999 Helmut Graupner wrote an article on pedophilia in the *Journal of Homosexuality,* in which he claims: "Man/boy and woman/girl relations without doubt are same-sex relations and they do constitute an aspect of gay and lesbian life." Graupner argues that, as such, consensual sexual relations between adult homosexuals and youths as young as fourteen qualifies as a "gay rights issue."

  Helmut Graupner, "Love Versus Abuse: Crossgenerational Sexual Relations of Minors: A Gay Rights Issue?" *Journal of Homosexuality* 37 (1999): 23, 26.

Voice of concern from within the homosexual community

The fascination with pedophilia has alarmed some within the gay community. Lesbian columnist Paula Martinac, writing in the homosexual newspaper *Washington Blade,* states:

- "[S]ome gay men still maintain that an adult who has same-sex relations with someone under the legal age of consent is on some level doing the kid a favor by helping to bring him or her 'out.' It's not pedophilia, this thinking goes—pedophilia refers only to *little* kids. Instead, adult-youth sex is viewed as an important aspect of gay culture, with a history dating back to 'Greek love' of ancient times. This romanticized version of adult-youth sexual relations has been a staple of gay literature and has made appearances, too, in gay-themed films."

Paula Martinac, "Mixed Messages on Pedophilia Need to be Clarified, Unified," *Washington Blade* (March 15, 2002).

- Martinac adds that "When some gay men venerate adult-youth sex as affirming while simultaneously declaring 'We're not pedophiles,' they send an inconsistent message to society....The lesbian and gay community will never be successful in fighting the pedophile stereo-type until we all stop condoning sex with young people."

Ibid.

The Consequences of Homosexual Child Abuse

Perhaps the most tragic aspect of the homosexual-pedophile connection is the fact that men who sexually molest boys all too often lead their victims into homosexuality and pedophilia.

Victims of child sexual abuse are more likely to become homosexual

- The *Archives of Sexual Behavior* reports: "One of the most salient findings of this study is that 46 percent of homosexual men and 22 percent of homosexual women reported having been molested by a person of the same gender. This contrasts to only 7 percent of heterosexual men and 1 percent of heterosexual women reporting having been molested by a person of the same gender."

Marie, E. Tomeo, et al., "Comparative Data of Childhood and Adolescence Molestation in Heterosexual and Homosexual Persons," *Archives of Sexual Behavior* 30 (2001): 539.

- A study of 279 homosexual/bisexual men with AIDS and control patients discussed in the *Journal of the American Medical Association* reported: "More than half of both case and control patients reported a sexual act with a male by age 16 years, approximately 20 percent by age 10 years."

  Harry W. Haverkos, et al., "The Initiation of Male Homosexual Behavior," *The Journal of the American Medical Association* 262 (July 28, 1989): 501.

- Noted child sex-abuse expert David Finkelhor found that "boys victimized by older men were over four times more likely to be currently engaged in homosexual activity than were non-victims. The finding applied to nearly half the boys who had had such an experience....Further, the adolescents themselves often linked their homosexuality to their sexual victimization experiences."

  Watkins & Bentovim, "The Sexual Abuse of Male Children and Adolescents," 316.

- The *Journal of Adolescent Health Care* reported a study of adolescent males who visited a health clinic and reported on a survey that they had been "raped, sexually abused, or forced to engage in a sexual act" prior to puberty. The authors noted, "The study group identified themselves as currently homosexual nearly seven times as often and bisexual nearly six times as often as the control group."

  Robert L. Johnson, M.D. and Diane K. Shrier, M.D., "Sexual Victimization of Boys: Experience at an Adolescent Medicine Clinic," *Journal of Adolescent Health Care* 6 (1985): 374.

Victims of child sexual abuse are more likely to become pedophiles

- A study in the *International Journal of Offender Therapy and Comparative Criminology* found: "In the case of childhood sexual experiences prior to the age of fourteen, 40 percent (of the pedophile sample) reported that they had engaged 'very often' in sexual activity with an adult, with 28 percent stating that this type of activity had occurred 'sometimes'"

  Gary A. Sawle, Jon Kear-Colwell, "Adult Attachment Style and Pedophilia: A Developmental Perspective," *International Journal of Offender Therapy and Comparative Criminology* 45 (February 2001): 6.

- A *National Institute of Justice* report states that "the odds that a childhood sexual abuse victim will be arrested as an adult for any sex crime is 4.7 times higher than for people . . . who experienced no victimization as children."

Cathy Spatz Widom, "Victims of Childhood Sexual Abuse—Later Criminal Consequences," *Victims of Childhood Sexual Abuse Series: NIJ Research in Brief,* (March 1995): 6.

- A *Child Abuse and Neglect* study found that 59 percent of male child sex offenders had been "victim of contact sexual abuse as a child."

Elliott, "Child Sexual Abuse Prevention: What Offenders Tell Us," 582.

- The *Journal of Child Psychiatry* noted that "there is a tendency among boy victims to recapitulate their own victimization, only this time with themselves in the role of perpetrator and someone else the victim."

Watkins & Bentovim, "The Sexual Abuse of Male Children and Adolescents," 319. The authors mention several studies confirming that between 19 percent and 61 percent of male sex abusers had previously been sexually abused themselves.

The overlapping of future homosexuality and future pedophilia as consequences of child sexual abuse simply reinforces the fact that the similar overlap in the nature of the abuse itself is no coincidence.

The Family Research Council

Founded in 1983, the Family Research Council is a nonprofit research and educational organization dedicated to articulating and advancing a family-centered philosophy of public life. In addition to providing research and analysis for the legislative, executive, and judicial branches of the federal government, the Council seeks to inform the news media, the academic community, business leaders, and the public about family issues that affect the nation. Among its efforts to educate citizens for responsible engagement in public life is the Witherspoon Fellowship, a civic and cultural leadership program for college students.

The Family Research council relies solely on the generosity of individuals, families, foundations and businesses for financial support. The Internal Revenue Service recognizes FRC as a tax-exempt, 501(c)(3) charitable organization. Donations are therefore tax-deductible in accordance with Section 170 of the Internal Revenue Code.

Located at 801 G Street, N.W., Washington, D.C., the headquarters of the Family Research Council provides its staff with strategic access to government decision-making centers, national media offices, and information sources. Owned by Faith Family Freedom, L.L.C., the six-story building was completed in 1996 through the generosity of the Edgar Prince and the Richard DeVos families of western Michigan. Visitors are welcome during normal business hours. Please call (202) 393-2100 in advance to ensure a pleasant and productive visit.